ARCTIC OCEAN

Queen
Elizabeth
Islands

Ellesmere
Island

Greenland

East Siberian
Sea

Beaufort Sea

Banks
Island

Baffin
Bay

Chukchi
Sea

Brooks Range

Mackenzie

Victoria
Island

Baffin Island

Davis Strait

Kolyma
Range

Yukon

Mount McKinley
(Denali)
6194m

Mackenzie
Mountains

Great Bear Lake

Great Slave Lake

Hudson
Bay

Labrador
Sea

Bering
Sea

Alaska Range

Coast Mountains

Rocky Mountains

NORTH
AMERICA

Canadian Shield

Kamchatka
Peninsula

Gulf of
Alaska

Aleutian Islands

Queen Charlotte
Islands

Vancouver Island

Lake
Winnipeg

Newfoundland

PACIFIC

OCEAN

Great
Basin

Great Plains

Missouri

Great Lakes

Nova Scotia

Colorado

Ohio

Appalachian Mts.

ATLANTIC

OCEAN

Rio Grande

Mississippi

Bermuda

Midway
Islands

Hawaiian Islands

Sierra Madre Occidental

Sierra Madre Oriental

Gulf of
Mexico

Bahamas

Hawaii

Cuba

West Indies

Greater Antilles

Marshall Islands

cronesia

ne
ds

Tungaru

Line Islands

Caribbean
Sea

Lesser Antilles

Melanesia

Llanos

Orinoco

Guiana
Highlands

Solomon Islands

Polynesia

Marquesas
Islands

Galapagos
Islands

Amazon

Amazon

Vanuatu

Fiji

Samoa

Cook Islands

Tuamotu Islands

Basin

SOUTH
AMERICA

New
Caledonia

Tonga

Pitcairn
Islands

PACIFIC

OCEAN

Andes

Paraguay

Brazilian Highlands

Austral
Islands

Easter Island

Gran Chaco

Paraguay

szko

Tasman
Sea

North
Island

Chatham Islands

Juan Fernandez
Islands

Cerro Aconcagua
6962m

Paraná

Uruguay

nia

South
Island

New
Zealand

Pampas

ATLANTIC

OCEAN

Patagonia

Andes

Falkland Islands

Tierra
del Fuego

Cape Horn

South Georgia

South Sandwich
Islands

SOUTHERN OCEAN

Antarctic
Peninsula

SCHOLASTIC CANADA

# Children's
# Atlas

# of the
# World

**Scholastic Canada Ltd.**
604 King Street West, Toronto, Ontario M5V 1E1, Canada

**Scholastic Inc.**
557 Broadway, New York, NY 10012, USA

**Scholastic Australia Pty Limited**
PO Box 579, Gosford, NSW 2250, Australia

**Scholastic New Zealand Limited**
Private Bag 94407, Greenmount, Auckland, New Zealand

**Scholastic Children's Books**
Euston House, 24 Eversholt Street, London NW1 1DB, UK

www.scholastic.ca

Cartography:
Digital Cartography supplied by Encompass Graphics Ltd, Hove, U.K.
Cartographic Consultant: Roger Bullen
Editorial Direction: Christiane Gunzi
Senior Editor: Louise Pritchard
Editorial Assistant: Katy Rayner
Art Direction: Chez Picthall
Design: Gillian Shaw and Paul Calver
Picture Research: Gillian Shaw and Katy Rayner
Map Indexing: Roger Bullen and Paula Metcalf
General Indexer: Angie Hipkin
Written by: Chez Picthall & Christiane Gunzi

Created and produced by Picthall & Gunzi, an imprint of Award Publications Limited.
This edition published 2015 by Scholastic Canada Ltd.

Library and Archives Canada Cataloguing in Publication

Picthall, Chez, author
Scholastic Canada children's atlas of the world / written by
Chez Picthall & Christiane Gunzi.
Originally published 2009.
ISBN 978-1-4431-4668-5 (bound)
1. Children's atlases. I. Gunzi, Christiane, author II. Title.
III. Title: Children's atlas of the world.
G1021.P52 2015          j912          C2014-908319-X

6  5  4  3  2  1          Printed in Malaysia  CP157          15  16  17  18  19

SCHOLASTIC CANADA

# Children's Atlas of the World

## Chez Picthall

SCHOLASTIC CANADA LTD.

New York  Toronto  London  Auckland  Sydney
Mexico City  New Delhi  Hong Kong  Buenos Aires

# Contents

## South America

## North America

## Africa

# Europe

# Oceania and the Pacific Islands

# Asia

# The Arctic and Antarctica

# All about maps

Maps show us what places on Earth look like from above. They give useful information, such as where towns and cities are, or where rivers and mountains run. A map can help us to find out where we are and can show us the distances between places. Maps have to carry a lot of information, so different symbols, lines and colours are used to show the features on the Earth's surface. Symbols are often used to show the position of towns, and lines show where all the country borders and rivers are.

A street m

A country m

**Map scales** Maps are large- or small-scale. Large-scale maps show small areas with lots of det like the street map above. Small-scale maps show large areas with less detail, like this country map. A the maps in this atlas are small-scale.

## How maps are made

The most accurate world maps are globes because they are the same shape as planet Earth. To make a flat map out of a globe, map-makers have to change the shape of Earth's surface. The land shapes get stretched and distorted. Map-makers do this work mathematically, using what is called a "projection." There are many different kinds of projection, and each one looks slightly different. The people who create maps are called "cartographers."

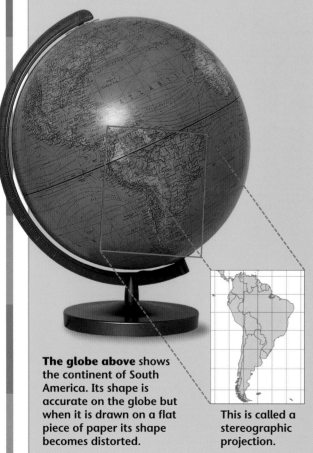

**The globe above** shows the continent of South America. Its shape is accurate on the globe but when it is drawn on a flat piece of paper its shape becomes distorted.

This is called a stereographic projection.

## Latitude and longitude lines

To help us to locate places, we have invented invisible lines that run around the Earth. These are called the lines of latitude and longitude. Lines of latitude run horizontally. They measure how far north or south a place is from the Equator (around the Earth's middle). Longitude lines run from the North to the South Pole and measure how far east or west a place is from Greenwich, London. All these measurements are given in degrees and show a place's position on Earth.

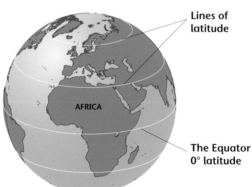

Lines of latitude

AFRICA

The Equator 0° latitude

Greenwich, London, UK 0° longitude

AFRICA

Lines of longitude

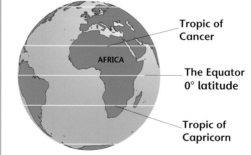

Tropic of Cancer

AFRICA

The Equator 0° latitude

Tropic of Capricorn

## The Equator and the Tropics

The Equator is an imaginary line that runs around the centre of the Earth. It is an equal distance from the North and South Poles. Lying parallel to the Equator are lines called the Tropics of Cancer and Capricorn. Between these lines the climate and land are tropical.

## North and South Poles

The North and South Poles are the most northerly and southerly points on the surface of the Earth. They are invisible and are found where all the lines of longitude meet. If you stood on the South Pole every direction would be north, and at the North Pole all directions would be south! There is no land at the North Pole, just the frozen waters of the Arctic Ocean.

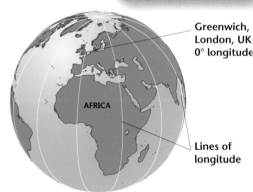

North Pole

AFRICA

AFRICA

South Pole

# How to use this atlas

The maps in this atlas have been arranged by continent in the following order: North America, South America, Africa, Europe, Asia, Oceania and Antarctica. Every map has a double page and the countries on each map are listed at the top left-hand side for easy reference. The Antarctic is shown with the Arctic, after all the other maps. Every map is accompanied by photographs of landscapes, wildlife, industries, famous landmarks, typical foods and interesting facts, to give you a snapshot of each area.

## The indexes

This atlas has two indexes. One index gives a list of all the place names shown on the maps. The other index lists the animals, industries, and other topics in the book. To find out how to use the indexes, see p. 60.

Index to place names

**Regional heading** tells you which region or country the map shows.

**Continent heading** tells you which continent the region is in.

**Introductory text** sets the scene for each map, giving general information about the region.

**Did you know?** boxes give you some fascinating facts about the countries on each of the maps.

**Locator globe** shows you which region of the world the map covers.

**Country Index** lists all the countries shown on the map.

**Grid letters and numbers** help you to find the cities, towns, rivers, mountains and other features listed in the index to the place names.

**Photographs** of animals, people and places help to bring the map to life.

**Flags** of each nation are shown next to their country.

**Compass rose** shows the direction of north for each map.

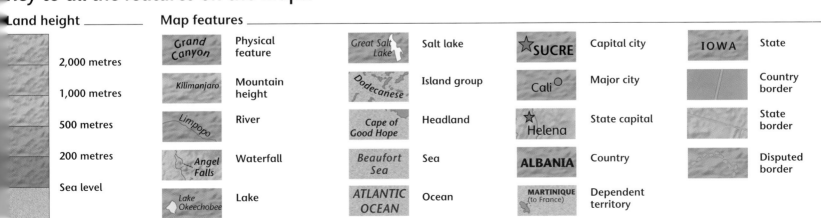

**Scale bar** helps you to work out the distances between places and how big countries are.

**Map colours** show you how high the land is.

**Quiz questions** test your map skills and understanding of topics featured on the page.

## Key to all the features on the maps:

| Land height | Map features | | | | | | | |
|---|---|---|---|---|---|---|---|---|
| 2,000 metres | Grand Canyon | Physical feature | Great Salt Lake | Salt lake | ☆SUCRE | Capital city | IOWA | State |
| 1,000 metres | Kilimanjaro | Mountain height | Dodecanese | Island group | Cali○ | Major city | | Country border |
| 500 metres | Limpopo | River | Cape of Good Hope | Headland | ☆ Helena | State capital | | State border |
| 200 metres | Angel Falls | Waterfall | Beaufort Sea | Sea | ALBANIA | Country | | Disputed border |
| Sea level | Lake Okeechobee | Lake | ATLANTIC OCEAN | Ocean | MARTINIQUE (to France) | Dependent territory | | |

# Our planet in space

If we wrote down the address for planet Earth it would be: Earth, The Solar System, The Milky Way, The Universe. Earth belongs to the Solar System, which forms just a tiny part of the Milky Way galaxy. A galaxy is a massive group of hundreds of billions of stars. The Milky Way is one of billions of galaxies in the Universe. The Universe is the name that we give to the whole of space.

## The Milky Way

Our Sun is one of 200 billion stars in the Milky Way. The Milky Way is a spiral galaxy and it is really enormous. It would take 100,000 light years to travel across it!

## The Solar System

Our Solar System is made up of the Sun and the eight planets and other bodies (such as comets, moons and asteroids) that orbit around it. The Sun is a star. Its powerful gravity keeps everything orbiting around it. The four planets that are nearest to the Sun (Mercury, Venus, Earth and Mars) are made of rock and metal. The four outer planets (Jupiter, Saturn, Uranus and Neptune) are mostly gas or liquid. They are known as the gas giants.

## Saturn

This planet is surrounded by many rings. These rings are a few hundred metres thick and about 270,000 kilometres in diameter. They are formed from millions of icy particles. The ice particles range in size from tiny pieces a few millimetres across to huge lumps that are tens of metres across.

## Pluto

Pluto used to be called a planet. But in 2006 the International Astronomical Union decided that it is only a dwarf planet.

## Neptune

This is the furthest planet from the Sun. A French mathematician discovered its existence in 1843 by doing calculations, but it was not actually seen for another three years.

## Uranus

The blue colour of Uranus comes from the gas called methane, which is in its atmosphere. Scientists think that this planet is made of different icy materials (methane, water and ammonia) surrounding a solid core.

### Did you know?

◇ Distances in space are measured in "light years." That is the distance that light travels in one year: 9.46 trillion kilometres!

## The relative distance of the planets from the Sun

**Neptune**
This is about 4.5 billion km from the Sun.

**Uranus**

**Saturn**

**Jupiter**

**Sun**

**Venus**

**Earth**

**Mars**

**Mercury**

## The Sun

The Sun is about 4.5 billion years old and is only half-way through its life. It is 1.4 million kilometres across and is made mostly of the gases hydrogen and helium. The temperature at its surface is 5,500°C.

### The Moon
Earth's Moon is made of solid rock. It is covered in craters made by meteorites that crashed into it.

### Mercury
The planet that is closest to the Sun is Mercury. This means that it has the shortest year (the time that it takes to go once round the Sun) of all the planets.

### Venus
The planet Venus is the brightest object in our night sky, after the Moon. This is because its atmosphere reflects more sunlight than any other planet.

### Earth
Earth is the third planet from the Sun and, as far as we know, it is the only planet in our Solar System that has any kind of life on it.

### Mars
Bright red dust covers most of the planet Mars. The dust often blows into fierce sandstorms. When this happens, the surface of the planet cannot be seen.

### Jupiter
This giant planet is made almost entirely of gas. Jupiter is the largest planet in the Solar System and it is 11 times larger in diameter than Earth.

### Did you know?

To qualify as a planet, a body must:
1) Orbit around a sun.
2) Be big enough for its own gravity to have pulled it into a ball.
3) Have cleared other bodies out of its orbit.

---

## Planet Earth's many layers

The rocky layer of Earth that we live on is called the crust. It is about 40 kilometres thick. Scientists believe that the inner core of Earth is solid iron. This is surrounded by a molten layer of iron and nickel, which is called the outer core. Between the Earth's outer core and its crust is the mantle.

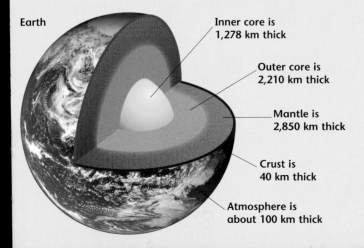

Earth

Inner core is 1,278 km thick

Outer core is 2,210 km thick

Mantle is 2,850 km thick

Crust is 40 km thick

Atmosphere is about 100 km thick

## When the surface of the Earth moves

Earth's crust is made up of tectonic plates, which are constantly moving and pushing past each other. Most of the time the movements are so small that we do not notice them. But sometimes, during an earthquake or a volcanic eruption, the Earth moves violently and these movements are easy to notice.

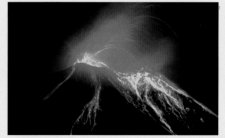

### Earthquake
When tectonic plates stick together instead of sliding past each other, stress builds up in the rocks until they crack or "fault." This cracking sends shock waves through the Earth, causing an earthquake. Powerful earthquakes can sometimes destroy whole cities.

### Volcano
Where the Earth's crust is weak, or at the point between two tectonic plates, magma (molten rock) seeps out and volcanoes can develop over time. The pressure of magma pushing up to the Earth's surface can be so powerful that a volcano will erupt, spewing out lava.

# Physical features of the world

Greenland

Greenland Sea

Spitsbergen

Franz Josef Land

Severnaya Zemlya

New Siberi Islands

Kara Sea

Laptev Sea

Taymyr Peninsula

Novaya Zemlya

North Siberian Lowland

Barents Sea

Norwegian Sea

Arctic Circle

Denmark Strait

Iceland

Faeroe Islands

Pechora

Ob'

West Siberian Plain

Central Siberian Plateau

S i b e r i a

Verkhoyanskiy Khrebet

Se

Ok

Sakh

Yenisey

Lena

Northern Dvina

Scandinavia

Lake Onega

Lake Ladoga

North Sea

Great Britain

Ireland

Baltic Sea

Volga

North European Plain

Ural Mountains

Ob

Lena

Angara

Yenisey

Lake Baikal

Altai Mountains

Aldan

Amur

A S I A

Manchurian Plain

ATLANTIC OCEAN

EUROPE

Rhine

Loire

Alps

Carpathian Mountains

Dnieper

Don

Danube

Black Sea

Volga

Caspian Sea

Caucasus
El'brus 5642m

Aral Sea

Lake Balkhash

Irtysh

Tien Shan

Takla Makan Desert

Gobi

Sea of Japan

Honsh

Iberian Peninsula

Azores

Mediterranean Sea

Anatolia

Tigris

Euphrates

Iranian Plateau

Zagros Mountains

Amu Darya

Hindu Kush

Himalayas

Plateau of Tibet

Yellow River

Great Plain of China

Yellow Sea

Shikoku

Kyushu

Atlas Mountains

The Gulf

Indus

Thar Desert

Ganges

Brahmaputra

Mount Everest 8848m

Yangtze

East China Sea

Tropic of Cancer

Canary Islands

Libyan Desert

Nile

Red Sea

Arabian Peninsula

Arabian Sea

Deccan

Xi Jiang

Taiwan

Philippine Sea

Mariana Islands

Sahara Desert

Sahel

Lake Chad

Bay of Bengal

Irrawaddy

Salween

M

Cape Verde Islands

Senegal

Niger

Blue Nile

Gulf of Aden

Laccadive Islands

Andaman Islands

Mekong

South China Sea

Philippine Islands

White Nile

Ethiopian Highlands

AFRICA

Great Rift Valley

Nicobar Islands

Malay Peninsula

Celebes Sea

Ce
Is

Equator

Gulf of Guinea

Ubangi

Congo

Congo Basin

Great Rift Valley

Lake Victoria

Kilimanjaro 5895m

Lake Tanganyika

Seychelles

Chagos Archipelago

Maldive Islands

Sri Lanka

Sumatra

East Indies

Java Sea

Sulawesi

New Guinea

Borneo

Java

Ascension Island

Lake Nyasa

Comoros Islands

Timor

Arafura Sea

St Helena

Namib Desert

Zambezi

Madagascar

Mozambique Channel

Mauritius

Réunion

Cocos Islands

INDIAN OCEAN

Great Sandy Desert

Simpson Desert

AUSTRALIA

Tropic of Capricorn

ATLANTIC OCEAN

Kalahari Desert

Orange River

Nullarbor Plain

Dari

Great Australian Bight

Mo
Kosciusz 222

Cape of Good Hope

Prince Edward Islands

Crozet Islands

Tasmania

Kerguelen

S O U T H E R N   O C E A N

Antarctic Circle

A N T A R C T I C A

30°    0°    30°    60°    90°    120°

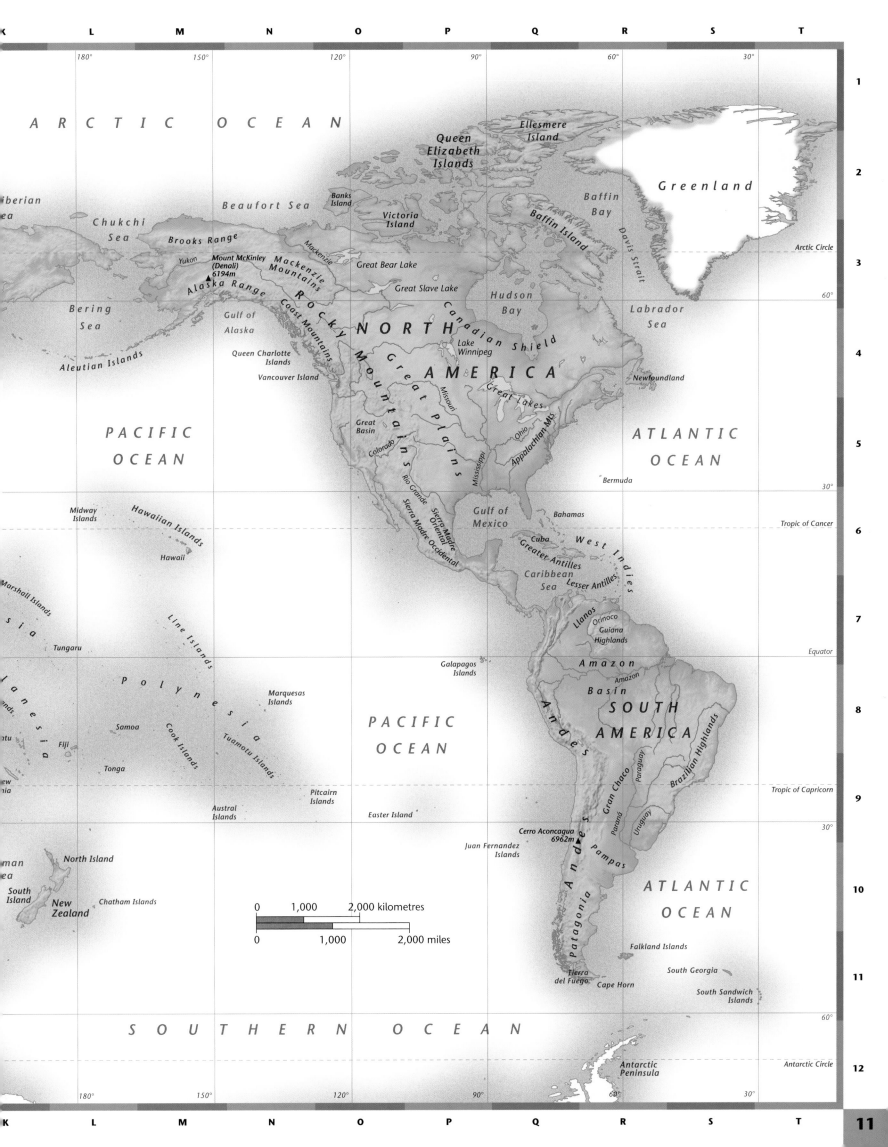

180°    150°    120°    90°    60°    30°

1

A R C T I C   O C E A N

Queen
Elizabeth
Islands

Ellesmere
Island

Greenland

2

iberian
ea

Chukchi
Sea

Beaufort Sea

Banks
Island

Victoria
Island

Baffin
Bay

Baffin Island

Arctic Circle

Brooks Range

Mackenzie
Mountains

Great Bear Lake

Davis Strait

60°

3

Yukon

Mount McKinley
(Denali)
6194m

Alaska Range

Coast Mountains

Mackenzie

Great Slave Lake

Hudson
Bay

Canadian Shield

Labrador
Sea

Bering
Sea

Gulf of
Alaska

Rocky

NORTH

Lake
Winnipeg

4

Aleutian Islands

Queen Charlotte
Islands

Vancouver Island

Great
Mountains

AMERICA

Great Lakes

Newfoundland

PACIFIC

Great
Basin

Great Plains

Missouri

Ohio

Appalachian Mts.

ATLANTIC

5

OCEAN

Colorado

Mississippi

OCEAN

Rio Grande

Bermuda

30°

Midway
Islands

Hawaiian Islands

Sierra Madre
Occidental

Sierra Madre
Oriental

Gulf of
Mexico

Bahamas

Tropic of Cancer

6

Hawaii

Cuba
Greater Antilles

West Indies

Caribbean
Sea

Lesser Antilles

Marshall Islands

Line Islands

Llanos

Orinoco
Guiana
Highlands

7

sia

Tungaru

Galapagos
Islands

Amazon

Amazon
Basin

Equator

Polynesia

Marquesas
Islands

SOUTH

8

lanesia

Samoa

Cook Islands

Tuamotu Islands

PACIFIC

Andes

AMERICA

Brazilian Highlands

ntu

Fiji

OCEAN

Tonga

Gran Chaco

Paraguay

Pitcairn
Islands

Tropic of Capricorn

9

ew
nia

Austral
Islands

Easter Island

Cerro Aconcagua
6962m

Parana

Uruguay

30°

Juan Fernandez
Islands

Pampas

North Island

ATLANTIC

10

man
ea

South
Island

New
Zealand

Chatham Islands

Andes

Patagonia

OCEAN

0    1,000    2,000 kilometres

0    1,000    2,000 miles

Falkland Islands

Tierra
del Fuego

Cape Horn

South Georgia

11

South Sandwich
Islands

60°

S O U T H E R N   O C E A N

12

Antarctic
Peninsula

Antarctic Circle

180°    150°    120°    90°    60°    30°

# Countries of the world

30° 0° 30° 60° 90° 120°

**GREENLAND**
(to Denmark)

**SVALBARD**
(to Norway)

**JAN MAYEN**
(to Norway)

Arctic Circle

**ICELAND**

**FAEROE ISLANDS**
(to Denmark)

60°

**ATLANTIC**

**OCEAN**

N O R W A Y

S W E D E N

**FINLAND**

R U S S I A N

**ISLE OF MAN**
(to UK)

**UNITED
KINGDOM**

**DENMARK**

**ESTONIA**
**LATVIA**
**LITHUANIA**

**RUSS.
FED.**

F E D E R A T I O N

**IRELAND**

**NETH.**
**BELG.**
**GERMANY**
**LUX.**
**LIECH.**

**POLAND**

**BELARUS**

**CHANNEL ISLANDS**
(to UK)

**FRANCE**

**SWITZ.**

**CZECH
REP.**
**SLOVAKIA**

**UKRAINE**

**KAZAKHSTAN**

**MONGOLIA**

**AUSTRIA**
**SLOV.**
**HUNGARY**

**MOLDOVA**

**MONACO**

**CROATIA**
**S.M.**

**ROMANIA**

**B&H**
**SERBIA**

**CRIMEA**
(disputed)

**GEORGIA**

**UZBEKISTAN**

**KYRGYZSTAN**

*Azores*
(to Portugal)

**ANDORRA**

**VATICAN CITY**

**MONT.**
**ALB.**

**BULGARIA**
**MACEDONIA**

**ARMENIA**
**AZERBAIJAN**

**TURKMENISTAN**

**TAJIKISTAN**

**NORTH
KOREA**

**PORTUGAL**
**SPAIN**

**ITALY**

**GREECE**

**TURKEY**

**AZER.**

**CHINA**

**SOUTH
KOREA**

**JAPAN**

**GIBRALTAR**
(to UK)

*Madeira*
(to Portugal)

**TUNISIA**

**MALTA**

**CYPRUS**
**LEBANON**
**ISRAEL**

**SYRIA**

**IRAQ**

**IRAN**

**AFGHANISTAN**

**Aksai Chin**
(Administered by China,
claimed by India)

30°

*Canary Islands*
(to Spain)

**MOROCCO**

**WESTERN
SAHARA**

**JORDAN**

**PAKISTAN**

**NEPAL**

**BHUTAN**

Tropic of Cancer

**ALGERIA**

**LIBYA**

**EGYPT**

**KUWAIT**

**BAHRAIN**

**QATAR**

**U.A.E.**

**SAUDI
ARABIA**

**BANGLADESH**

**BURMA
(MYANMAR)**

**TAIWAN**

**MAURITANIA**

**CAPE VERDE**

**MALI**

**NIGER**

**CHAD**

**INDIA**

**SENEGAL**

**GAMBIA**

**GUINEA-BISSAU**
**GUINEA**

**BURKINA
FASO**

**SUDAN**

**ERITREA**

**YEMEN**

**OMAN**

*Socotra*
(to Yemen)

*Laccadive
Islands*
(to India)

*Andaman &
Nicobar
Islands*
(to India)

**NORTH
MARIANA
ISL.**
(to US)

**GUAM**
(to US)

**PARACEL
ISLANDS**
(disputed)

**PHILIPPINES**

**SIERRA LEONE**

**LIBERIA**

**IVORY
COAST**

**GHANA**

**BENIN**

**NIGERIA**

**CENTRAL
AFRICAN
REPUBLIC**

**SOUTH
SUDAN**

**ETHIOPIA**

**DJIBOUTI**

**SOMALIA**

**SRI
LANKA**

**MALDIVES**

**THAILAND**

**LAOS**

**VIETNAM**

**CAMBODIA**

**SPRATLY
ISLANDS**
(disputed)

**BRUNEI**

**MICRO**

**TOGO**

**CAMEROON**

**EQUATORIAL
GUINEA**

**UGANDA**

**KENYA**

**MALAYSIA**

**PALAU**

Equator

**SAO TOME & PRINCIPE**

**GABON**

**CONGO**

**DEMOCRATIC
REPUBLIC
OF CONGO**

**RWANDA**
**BURUNDI**

**SINGAPORE**

**I N D O N E S I A**

**ANGOLA**
(Cabinda)

**TANZANIA**

**SEYCHELLES**

**BRITISH INDIAN
OCEAN TERRITORY**
(to UK)

**CHRISTMAS ISLAND**
(to Australia)

**ASCENSION ISLAND**
(to St Helena)

**ANGOLA**

**ZAMBIA**

**MALAWI**

**COMOROS**

**MAYOTTE**
(to France)

**COCOS ISLANDS**
(to Australia)

**EAST TIMOR**

**ST HELENA**
(to UK)

**ZIMBABWE**

**MOZAMBIQUE**

**MADAGASCAR**

**RÉUNION**
(to France)

**MAURITIUS**

**INDIAN**

**NAMIBIA**

**BOTSWANA**

Tropic of Capricorn

**OCEAN**

**A U S T R A L I A**

30°

**ATLANTIC**

**SOUTH
AFRICA**

**SWAZILAND**

**LESOTHO**

**OCEAN**

| List of Abbreviations | |
|---|---|
| ALB. | Albania |
| BELG. | Belgium |
| B&H | Bosnia & Herzegovina |
| CZECH REP. | Czech Republic |
| LIECH. | Liechtenstein |
| LUX. | Luxembourg |
| MONT. | Montenegro |
| NETH. | Netherlands |
| NZ | New Zealand |
| SLOV. | Slovenia |
| S.M. | San Marino |
| SWITZ. | Switzerland |
| U.A.E. | United Arab Emirates |
| UK | United Kingdom |
| US | United States of America |

**FRENCH SOUTHERN &
ANTARCTIC TERRITORIES**
(to France)

*Prince Edward Islands*
(to South Africa)

**HEARD & MCDONALD ISLANDS**
(to Australia)

60°

S O U T H E R N   O C E A N

Antarctic Circle

12

30° 0° 30° 60° 90° 120°

A N T A R C T I C A

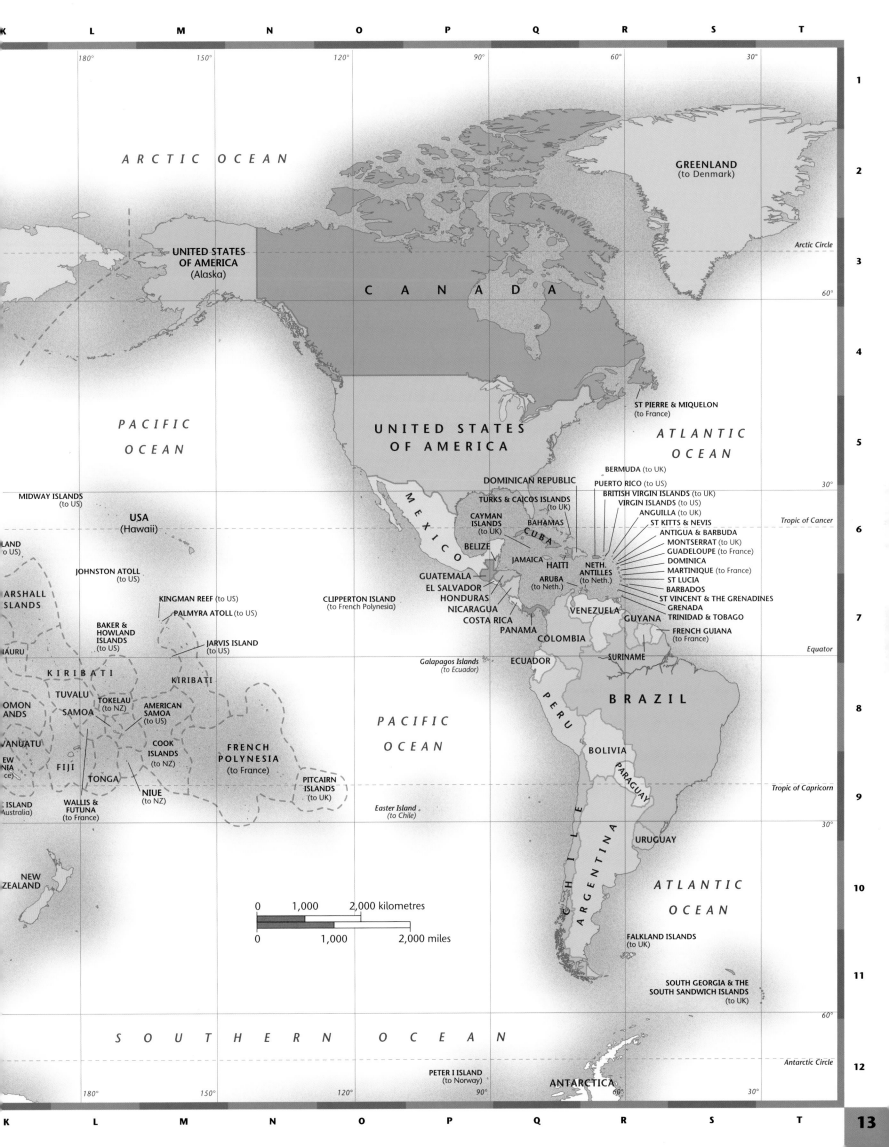

K L M N O P Q R S T

1

180° 150° 120° 90° 60° 30°

ARCTIC OCEAN

2

GREENLAND
(to Denmark)

Arctic Circle
3

UNITED STATES
OF AMERICA
(Alaska)

60°

C A N A D A

4

ST PIERRE & MIQUELON
(to France)

ATLANTIC
OCEAN
5

PACIFIC

OCEAN

UNITED STATES
OF AMERICA

BERMUDA (to UK)

DOMINICAN REPUBLIC

30°

PUERTO RICO (to US)

MIDWAY ISLANDS
(to US)

TURKS & CAICOS ISLANDS
(to UK)

BRITISH VIRGIN ISLANDS (to UK)

VIRGIN ISLANDS (to US)

ANGUILLA (to UK)

Tropic of Cancer

USA
(Hawaii)

MEXICO

CAYMAN
ISLANDS
(to UK)

BAHAMAS

ST KITTS & NEVIS

ANTIGUA & BARBUDA

MONTSERRAT (to UK)

LAND
o US)

BELIZE

CUBA

GUADELOUPE (to France)

DOMINICA

JOHNSTON ATOLL
(to US)

JAMAICA

HAITI

MARTINIQUE (to France)

GUATEMALA

NETH.
ANTILLES
(to Neth.)

ST LUCIA

ARSHALL
SLANDS

KINGMAN REEF (to US)

EL SALVADOR

ARUBA
(to Neth.)

BARBADOS

PALMYRA ATOLL (to US)

HONDURAS

ST VINCENT & THE GRENADINES

CLIPPERTON ISLAND
(to French Polynesia)

NICARAGUA

GRENADA

BAKER &
HOWLAND
ISLANDS
(to US)

COSTA RICA

VENEZUELA

TRINIDAD & TOBAGO

JARVIS ISLAND
(to US)

PANAMA

GUYANA

FRENCH GUIANA
(to France)

AURU

COLOMBIA

7

Equator

Galapagos Islands
(to Ecuador)

ECUADOR

SURINAME

KIRIBATI

KIRIBATI

TUVALU

TOKELAU
(to NZ)

PERU

BRAZIL

OMON
ANDS

SAMOA

AMERICAN
SAMOA
(to US)

8

VANUATU

COOK
ISLANDS
(to NZ)

FRENCH
POLYNESIA
(to France)

BOLIVIA

EW
NIA
ce)

FIJI

PACIFIC

OCEAN

PARAGUAY

TONGA

NIUE
(to NZ)

PITCAIRN
ISLANDS
(to UK)

Tropic of Capricorn

ISLAND
Australia)

WALLIS &
FUTUNA
(to France)

Easter Island
(to Chile)

30°
9

CHILE

URUGUAY

NEW
ZEALAND

ARGENTINA

ATLANTIC
10

0 1,000 2,000 kilometres

OCEAN

0 1,000 2,000 miles

FALKLAND ISLANDS
(to UK)

11

SOUTH GEORGIA & THE
SOUTH SANDWICH ISLANDS
(to UK)

60°

S O U T H E R N O C E A N

12

Antarctic Circle

PETER I ISLAND
(to Norway)

ANTARCTICA

180° 150° 120° 90° 60° 30°

K L M N O P Q R S T

13

# Climate and land cover

Climate is the average pattern of the weather over about 30 years. The climate of a place depends on how much sunshine and rain it gets, how close it is to the sea and sea currents, and how high it is above sea level. Different kinds of plants grow in different climates. The type of vegetation in an area, such as grassland or tropical forest, is called "land cover." Different land cover is suitable for different animals. The countries around the Equator get the most sunlight and rain. It is there that the habitats with the largest numbers of animals and plants are found. In places where there is little rainfall or the temperatures are too hot or cold, such as the Sahara or the North and South Poles, only a few species of plants and animals are able to survive.

**Temperate broadleaf forest**
Forests in temperate parts of the world have mild temperatures and plenty of rain. These forests contain trees such as oak, beech, birch and chestnut. Broadleaved trees collect nutrients in summer and shed their leaves in autumn to save energy and water.

**Tropical broadleaf forest**
Tropical forests that grow near the Equator have high temperatures and receive heavy rainfall all year round. The forests may contain over 50,000 different species of trees, as well as huge numbers of other plants and animals.

### Earth's changing climate
The world's climate is gradually changing, and this is having huge effects on its wildlife and people. Some areas have unusual floods and other places are affected by drought. Many kinds of animals, including polar bears, are threatened by climate change. Not all the animals and plants will be able to adapt to these new conditions.

**Did you know?**

◈ The different environments (habitats) on planet Earth where life exists are called biomes. A certain area, such as a forest or desert, is called an ecosystem.

### Extreme weather
Violent storms, heavy rainfall, strong winds and long periods of sunshine are all examples of extreme weather. Extreme weather often causes widespread flooding or drought, and the effects of these can be devastating. People may be killed or left homeless, and crops, farm animals and wildlife may be destroyed.

## Needleleaf forest

Stretching across northern parts of Asia, Europe and North America is a belt of tall, evergreen trees with needle-like leaves. They can survive cold winters because they gather nutrients all year.

## Cropland

Many of the most fertile areas of the world, especially Europe and North America, do not have their natural land cover. This has been cleared over hundreds of years to grow crops for food.

## Grassland

In areas of a continent where there is not enough rain for trees to grow, there are huge grasslands. These are called steppes and prairies in the north. In South America they are known as pampas.

## Tundra

Areas of tundra are mostly found near the Arctic Circle. The soil is frozen for much of the year. In places where it melts for a few months, plants such as lichens, mosses and low shrubs are able to grow.

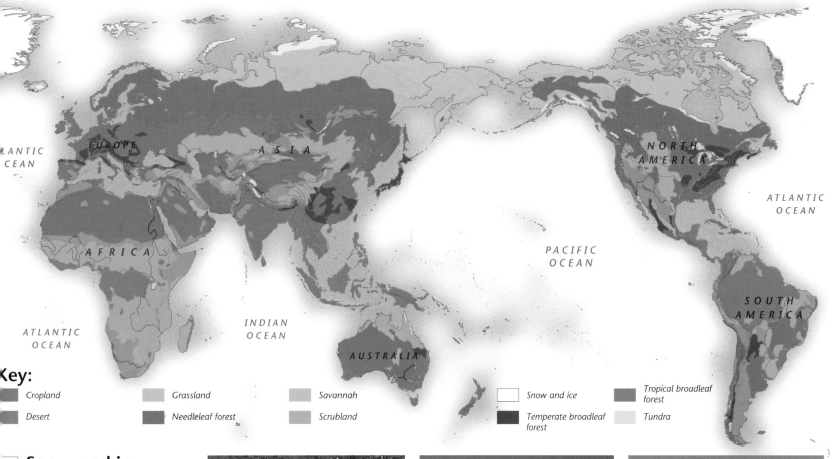

ATLANTIC OCEAN

EUROPE

ASIA

AFRICA

ATLANTIC OCEAN

INDIAN OCEAN

AUSTRALIA

PACIFIC OCEAN

NORTH AMERICA

ATLANTIC OCEAN

SOUTH AMERICA

Key:

- Cropland
- Desert
- Grassland
- Needleleaf forest
- Savannah
- Scrubland
- Snow and ice
- Temperate broadleaf forest
- Tropical broadleaf forest
- Tundra

## Snow and ice

In the Arctic and Antarctic, and on the highest parts of mountain ranges, such as the Alps and the Andes, there is snow and ice all year round. Temperatures remain well below freezing and it is often windy. Very few animals and plants can survive in such a harsh environment.

## Scrubland

At the edges of both hot and cold deserts there are areas of scrubland. Where it is too hot or too cold for trees to survive, tough, spiny shrubs with small leaves grow well.

## Desert

Deserts have very little water and are often windy. Few plants or animals can survive, as temperatures soar to over 40°C in the day and drop to below freezing at night.

## Savannah

Between hot deserts and tropical forests are areas called savannah. There is grass here and lots of trees, but the trees do not grow close together in big groups.

# Planet Earth's population

About 100 years ago, there were 1,625 million people on Earth, but in 2012 the world's population reached seven billion. Every second, our planet's population gets larger by two or three people. If this rate of growth continues there could be another billion people living on Earth in 12 to 13 years' time. People live in most parts of the world, but they are not evenly distributed. Some countries, such as Singapore, have dense populations with thousands of people for every square kilometre of land (which is called its population density), but others, such as Mongolia, have fewer than two people for every square kilometre. Most of the areas where hardly any people live are either too hot and dry, such as the Sahara, or too cold, such as the poles.

## Is there enough for everyone?

As the world's population continues to grow, more houses, food, water and fuel are needed. In some areas there is not enough clean water or shelter for everyone. Some countries cannot grow enough food, and do not have enough fuel supplies.

## World population

This map shows how the world's population is spread out. Most people live in South and East Asia. In 1900 only a few towns had more than 1 million people living in them. Now 20 of the world's cities have over 15 million people.

EUROPE has mostly warm summers and mild winters, and much of the land is fertile and easy to farm, which provides ideal living conditions.

AFRICA has the Sahara, which is the biggest desert in the world. Living here is difficult because the temperatures range from 50°C during the day to below 0°C at night. Most people living here belong to nomadic tribes.

SOUTH ASIA has the biggest, and one of the fastest-growing populations in the world. One-fifth of the world's population lives in this area.

RUSSIAN FEDERATION

Moscow

ATLANTIC OCEAN

London EUROPE

ASIA Beijing Seoul Tokyo Osaka

Cairo Delhi Shanghai

Karachi Dhaka

Mumbai Kolkata

AFRICA Manila

Jakarta

INDIAN OCEAN

AUSTRALIA

## Busy, busy cities

In the 1900s, only 1 out of every 10 people lived in a city. Now more than 5 out of 10 people live in cities. India and China have the most cities with over one million people, even though two-thirds of India's population live in the countryside. By 2030 almost two-thirds of the world's population may live in cities.

## Population growth

The world's population is more than six times bigger than it was 200 years ago. This is mostly due to better healthcare and improved ways of growing food and supplying clean water. A well-fed population with better healthcare means that more babies are being born alive and more of them survive, and people are living longer too.

**Did you know?**

◈ A country's population density is worked out by dividing the number of people in the country by the number of square kilometres of land.

**These are the most populated countries in the world.**

In 2014 there were 12 countries with national populations of more than 100,000,000 people.

| | | |
|---|---|---|
| 1 | China | 1,355,692,576 |
| 2 | India | 1,236,344,631 |
| 3 | USA | 318,892,103 |
| 4 | Indonesia | 253,609,643 |
| 5 | Brazil | 202,656,788 |
| 6 | Pakistan | 196,174,380 |
| 7 | Nigeria | 177,155,754 |
| 8 | Bangladesh | 166,280,712 |
| 9 | Russian Federation | 142,470,272 |
| 10 | Japan | 127,103,388 |
| 11 | Mexico | 120,286,655 |
| 12 | Philippines | 107,668,231 |

## Controlling the population

In some parts of the world people have large families. This can be because of religious beliefs, traditions or due to poverty. To help slow down population growth, many governments now teach people how to plan their families better. In China the government has ruled that couples may not have more than one child without permission.

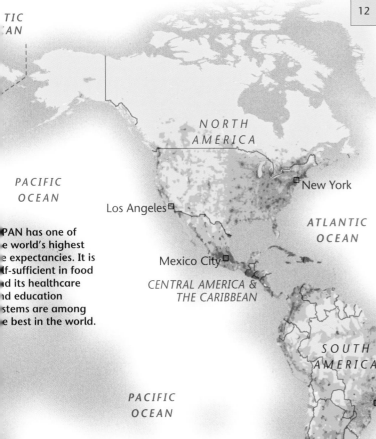

**Key to the map:**
People per square kilometre

More than 1,000
100–999
50–99
10–49
1–9
Less than 1

0 — 2,000 kilometres
0 — 2,000 miles

NORTH AMERICA
ARCTIC OCEAN
PACIFIC OCEAN
New York
Los Angeles
ATLANTIC OCEAN
Mexico City
CENTRAL AMERICA & THE CARIBBEAN
PACIFIC OCEAN
SOUTH AMERICA
São Paulo
Buenos Aires

JAPAN has one of the world's highest life expectancies. It is self-sufficient in food and its healthcare and education systems are among the best in the world.

**Did you know?**

◈ Monaco is the world's most densely populated country, with 16,000 people per square kilometre.

SOUTH AMERICA has a population that is mainly around the coast and in the northern parts of the Andes. The population in many towns has grown enormously because people have moved from the countryside to the towns to find work.

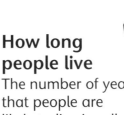

## How long people live

The number of years that people are likely to live is called their "life expectancy." People in different countries have different life expectancies. In countries where there is not enough food or clean water, people are not expected to live to an old age. Swaziland has a high amount of the HIV/AIDS disease, and life expectancy is 50 years. Japan is one of the richest countries and has the highest life expectancy, at almost 85 years. Andorra has the second-highest, at over 84 years.

# Flags and facts

All the countries in the world have their own national flag. Each flag is a colourful symbol of its country's people and government. The population of every country changes daily. Most countries have growing populations, although some decrease due to war, natural disasters, or political pressure. Below is a list of all the continents and countries. Each country's flag, capital city and population are included.

## NORTH AMERICA
**Canada p. 20**

**Canada**
Capital City Ottawa
Population 34,834,841

**USA p. 22**
**United States of America**
Capital City Washington DC
Population 318,892,103

**Central America and the Caribbean p. 24**
**Antigua and Barbuda**
Capital City St John's
Population 91,295

**Bahamas**
Capital City Nassau
Population 321,834

**Barbados**
Capital City Bridgetown
Population 289,680

**Belize**
Capital City Belmopan
Population 340,844

**Costa Rica**
Capital City San Jose
Population 4,755,234

**Cuba**
Capital City Havana
Population 11,047,251

**Dominica**
Capital City Roseau
Population 73,449

**Dominican Republic**
Capital City Santo Domingo
Population 10,349,741

**El Salvador**
Capital City San Salvador
Population 6,125,512

**Grenada**
Capital City St George's
Population 110,152

**Guatemala**
Capital City Guatemala City
Population 14,647,083

**Haiti**
Capital City Port-au-Prince
Population 9,996,731

**Honduras**
Capital City Tegucigalpa
Population 8,598,561

**Jamaica**
Capital City Kingston
Population 2,930,050

**Mexico**
Capital City Mexico City
Population 120,286,655

**Nicaragua**
Capital City Managua
Population 5,848,641

**Panama**
Capital City Panama City
Population 3,608,431

**St Lucia**
Capital City Castries
Population 163,362

**St Kitts and Nevis**
Capital City Basseterre
Population 51,538

**St Vincent and the Grenadines**
Capital City Kingstown
Population 102,918

**Trinidad and Tobago**
Capital City Port-of-Spain
Population 1,223,916

## SOUTH AMERICA
**South America p. 26**

**Argentina**
Capital City Buenos Aires
Population 43,024,374

**Bolivia**
Capital Cities La Paz and Sucre
Population 10,631,486

**Brazil**
Capital City Brasilia
Population 202,656,788

**Chile**
Capital City Santiago
Population 17,363,894

**Colombia**
Capital City Bogota
Population 46,245,297

**Ecuador**
Capital City Quito
Population 15,654,411

**Guyana**
Capital City Georgetown
Population 735,554

**Paraguay**
Capital City Asuncion
Population 6,703,860

**Peru**
Capital City Lima
Population 30,147,935

**Suriname**
Capital City Paramaribo
Population 573,311

**Uruguay**
Capital City Montevideo
Population 3,332,972

**Venezuela**
Capital City Caracas
Population 28,868,486

## AFRICA
**Northern Africa p. 28**

**Algeria**
Capital City Algiers
Population 38,813,722

**Benin**
Capital City Porto-Novo
Population 10,160,556

**Burkina Faso**
Capital City Ouagadougou
Population 18,365,123

**Cameroon**
Capital City Yaounde
Population 23,130,708

**Cape Verde**
Capital City Praia
Population 538,535

**Central African Republic**
Capital City Bangui
Population 5,277,959

**Chad**
Capital City Ndjamena
Population 11,412,107

**Djibouti**
Capital City Djibouti
Population 810,179

**Egypt**
Capital City Cairo
Population 86,895,099

**Eritrea**
Capital City Asmara
Population 6,380,803

**Ethiopia**
Capital City Addis Ababa
Population 96,633,458

**Gambia**
Capital City Banjul
Population 1,925,527

**Ghana**
Capital City Accra
Population 25,758,108

**Guinea**
Capital City Conakry
Population 11,474,383

**Guinea-Bissau**
Capital City Bissau
Population 1,693,398

**Ivory Coast**
Capital City Yamoussoukro
Population 22,848,945

**Liberia**
Capital City Monrovia
Population 4,092,310

**Libya**
Capital City Tripoli
Population 6,244,174

**Mali**
Capital City Bamako
Population 16,455,903

**Mauritania**
Capital City Nouakchott
Population 3,516,806

**Morocco**
Capital City Rabat
Population 32,987,206

**Niger**
Capital City Niamey
Population 17,466,172

**Nigeria**
Capital City Abuja
Population 177,155,754

**Senegal**
Capital City Dakar
Population 13,635,927

**Sierra Leone**
Capital City Freetown
Population 5,743,725

**Somalia**
Capital City Mogadishu
Population 10,428,043

**South Sudan**
Capital City Juba
Population 11,562,695

**Sudan**
Capital City Khartoum
Population 35,482,233

**Togo**
Capital City Lome
Population 7,351,374

**Tunisia**
Capital City Tunis
Population 10,937,521

**Western Sahara**
Capital City Laayoune
Population 554,795

**Southern Africa p. 30**

**Angola**
Capital City Luanda
Population 19,088,106

**Botswana**
Capital City Gaborone
Population 2,155,784

**Burundi**
Capital City Bujumbura
Population 10,395,931

**Comoros**
Capital City Moroni
Population 766,865

**Congo**
Capital City Brazzaville
Population 4,662,446

**Congo, DR**
Capital City Kinshasa
Population 77,433,744

**Equatorial Guinea**
Capital City Malabo
Population 722,254

**Gabon**
Capital City Libreville
Population 1,672,597

**Kenya**
Capital City Nairobi
Population 45,010,056

**Lesotho**
Capital City Maseru
Population 1,942,008

**Madagascar**
Capital City Antananarivo
Population 23,201,926

**Malawi**
Capital City Lilongwe
Population 17,377,468

**Mauritius**
Capital City Port Louis
Population 1,331,155

**Mozambique**
Capital City Maputo
Population 24,692,144

**Namibia**
Capital City Windhoek
Population 2,198,406

**Rwanda**
Capital City Kigali
Population 12,337,138

**São Tome and Principe**
Capital City Sao Tome
Population 190,428

**Seychelles**
Capital City Victoria
Population 91,650

**South Africa**
Capital Cities Bloemfontein, Cape Town and Tshwane (Pretoria)
Population 48,375,645

**Swaziland**
Capital City Mbabane
Population 1,419,623

**Tanzania**
Capital City Dodoma
Population 49,639,138

**Uganda**
Capital City Kampala
Population 35,918,915

**Zambia**
Capital City Lusaka
Population 14,638,505

**Zimbabwe**
Capital City Harare
Population 13,771,721

## EUROPE
**Northern Europe p. 3**

**Denmark**
Capital City Copenhagen
Population 5,569,077

**Estonia**
Capital City Tallinn
Population 1,257,921

**Finland**
Capital City Helsinki
Population 5,268,799

**Iceland**
Capital City Reykjavik
Population 317,351

**Latvia**
Capital City Riga
Population 2,165,165

**Lithuania**
Capital City Vilnius
Population 3,505,738

**Norway**
Capital City Oslo
Population 5,147,792

**Sweden**
Capital City Stockholm
Population 9,723,809

## Western Europe p. 34

**Andorra**
Capital City Andorra la Vella
Population 85,458

**Belgium**
Capital City Brussels
Population 10,449,361

**France**
Capital City Paris
Population 66,259,012

**Ireland**
Capital City Dublin
Population 4,832,765

**Luxembourg**
Capital City Luxembourg
Population 520,672

**Monaco**
Capital City Monaco-Ville
Population 30,508

**Netherlands**
Capital Cities Amsterdam and
The Hague
Population 16,877,351

**Portugal**
Capital City Lisbon
Population 10,813,834

**Spain**
Capital City Madrid
Population 47,737,941

**United Kingdom**
Capital City London
Population 63,742,977

## Central Europe p. 36

**Austria**
Capital City Vienna
Population 8,223,062

**Czech Republic**
Capital City Prague
Population 10,627,448

**Germany**
Capital City Berlin
Population 80,996,685

**Italy**
Capital City Rome
Population 61,680,122

**Liechtenstein**
Capital City Vaduz
Population 37,313

**Malta**
Capital City Valletta
Population 412,655

**Poland**
Capital City Warsaw
Population 38,346,279

**San Marino**
Capital City San Marino
Population 32,742

**Slovakia**
Capital City Bratislava
Population 5,443,583

**Slovenia**
Capital City Ljubljana
Population 1,988,292

**Switzerland**
Capital City Bern
Population 8,061,516

**Vatican City**
Capital City Vatican City
Population 842

## Southeast Europe p. 38

**Albania**
Capital City Tirana
Population 3,020,209

**Belarus**
Capital City Minsk
Population 9,608,058

**Bosnia and Herzegovina**
Capital City Sarajevo
Population 3,871,643

**Bulgaria**
Capital City Sofia
Population 6,924,716

**Croatia**
Capital City Zagreb
Population 4,470,534

**Greece**
Capital City Athens
Population 10,775,557

**Hungary**
Capital City Budapest
Population 9,919,128

**Kosovo**
Capital City Pristina
Population 1,859,203

**Macedonia**
Capital City Skopje
Population 2,091,719

**Moldova**
Capital City Chisinau
Population 3,583,288

**Montenegro**
Capital City Podgorica
Population 650,036

**Romania**
Capital City Bucharest
Population 21,729,871

**Serbia**
Capital City Belgrade
Population 7,209,764

**Ukraine**
Capital City Kiev
Population 44,291,413

## Russian Federation p. 40

**Russian Federation**
Capital City Moscow
Population 142,470,272

## ASIA
### Southwest Asia p. 42

**Armenia**
Capital City Yerevan
Population 3,060,631

**Azerbaijan**
Capital City Baku
Population 9,686,210

**Bahrain**
Capital City Manama
Population 1,314,089

**Cyprus**
Capital City Nicosia
Population 1,172,458

**Georgia**
Capital City T'bilisi
Population 4,935,880

**Iran**
Capital City Tehran
Population 80,840,713

**Iraq**
Capital City Baghdad
Population 32,585,692

**Israel**
Capital City Jerusalem
Population 7,821,850

**Jordan**
Capital City Amman
Population 7,930,491

**Kuwait**
Capital City Kuwait
Population 2,742,711

**Lebanon**
Capital City Beirut
Population 5,882,562

**Oman**
Capital City Muscat
Population 3,219,775

**Qatar**
Capital City Doha
Population 2,123,160

**Saudi Arabia**
Capital City Riyadh
Population 27,345,986

**Syria**
Capital City Damascus
Population 17,951,639

**Turkey**
Capital City Ankara
Population 81,619,392

**United Arab Emirates**
Capital City Abu Dhabi
Population 5,628,805

**Yemen**
Capital City Sana
Population 26,052,966

## Central Asia p. 44

**Afghanistan**
Capital City Kabul
Population 31,822,848

**Kazakhstan**
Capital City Astana
Population 17,948,816

**Kyrgyzstan**
Capital City Bishkek
Population 5,604,212

**Tajikistan**
Capital City Dushanbe
Population 8,051,512

**Turkmenistan**
Capital City Asgabat
Population 8,051,512

**Uzbekistan**
Capital City Tashkent
Population 28,929,716

## South Asia p. 46

**Bangladesh**
Capital City Dhaka
Population 166,280,712

**Bhutan**
Capital City Thimphu
Population 733,643

**India**
Capital City New Delhi
Population 1,236,344,631

**Maldives**
Capital City Male
Population 393,595

**Nepal**
Capital City Kathmandu
Population 30,986,975

## East Asia p. 48

**China**
Capital City Beijing
Population 1,355,692,576

**Japan**
Capital City Tokyo
Population 127,103,388

**Mongolia**
Capital City Ulan Bator
Population 2,953,190

**North Korea**
Capital City Pyongyang
Population 24,851,627

**South Korea**
Capital City Seoul
Population 49,039,986

**Taiwan**
Capital City Taipei
Population 23,359,928

## Southeast Asia p. 50

**Brunei**
Capital City Bandar Seri Begawan
Population 422,675

**Burma**
Capital City Naypyidaw
Population 55,746,253

**Cambodia**
Capital City Phnom Penh
Population 15,458,332

**East Timor**
Capital City Dili
Population 1,201,542

**Indonesia**
Capital City Jakarta
Population 253,609,643

**Laos**
Capital City Vientiane
Population 6,803,699

**Malaysia**
Capital City Kuala Lumpur
Population 30,073,353

**Philippines**
Capital City Manila
Population 107,668,231

**Singapore**
Capital City Singapore
Population 5,567,301

**Pakistan**
Capital City Islamabad
Population 196,174,380

**Sri Lanka**
Capital City Colombo
Population 21,866,445

## AUSTRALASIA AND OCEANIA
### Australia p. 52

**Australia**
Capital City Canberra
Population 22,507,617

## Pacific Islands p. 54

**Fiji**
Capital City Suva
Population 903,207

**Kiribati**
Capital City Bairiki
Population 104,488

**Marshall Islands**
Capital City Majuro
Population 70,983

**Micronesia**
Capital City Palikir
Population 105,681

**Nauru**
Capital City no official capital
Population 9,488

**Palau**
Capital City Ngerulmud (Melekeok)
Population 21,186

**Papua New Guinea**
Capital City Port Moresby
Population 6,552,730

**Samoa**
Capital City Apia
Population 196,628

**Solomon Islands**
Capital City Honiara
Population 609,883

**Tonga**
Capital City Nuku'alofa
Population 106,440

**Tuvalu**
Capital City Funafuti
Population 10,782

**Vanuatu**
Capital City Port-Vila
Population 266,937

## New Zealand p. 56

**New Zealand**
Capital City Wellington
Population 4,401,916

## ANTARCTICA p. 59

The continent of Antarctica is unusual because it does not have any countries.

**Thailand**
Capital City Bangkok
Population 67,741,401

**Vietnam**
Capital City Ha Noi
Population 93,421,835

# Canada

NORTH AMERICA

Canada is the second-largest country in the world
It is part of North America. Wheat and other crops grow
on the Great Plains. Farther north are thick coniferous
forests and many rivers and lakes. Near the Arctic
Circle, in the north, is a huge area of tundra, which turns
marshy in summer. Inside the Arctic Circle the ground is
always frozen. Most of the 35 million Canadian people
live in the south, within 160 kilometres of the border
with the USA. The weather is milder there and
travelling is easier. Canada's multicultural
population includes more than a million
aboriginal people. Canada is rich in
minerals and fossil fuels, and mining is
an important industry. Other industries
are fishing, agriculture, timber, and
machinery, car and paper manufacturing.

**Country File**

Canada

The maple leaf
is the national
symbol of Canada.

ARCTIC OCEAN

Qu

Beaufort
Sea

Banks
Island

UNITED STATES OF AMERICA
(Alaska)

Arctic Circle

Victo
Islar

Yukon

MACKENZIE MOUNTAINS

Great Bear
Lake

YUKON
TERRITORY

NORTHWEST
TERRITORIES

Mount Logan
5959m ▲

Whitehorse

Mackenzie

Yellowknife

Great Slave
Lake

C

ROCKY MOUNTAINS

A

Z

Lake
Athabasca

Peace

Queen
Charlotte
Islands

Reindeer
Lake

BRITISH

C

ALBERTA

GREAT

Prince George

SASKATCHEWA

Athabasca

Edmonton

COLUMBIA

Fraser

Red
Deer

P

Saskatche

Vancouver
Island

Kamloops

Calgary

L

Saskatoon

Vancouver

Nanaimo

Kelowna

A

Victoria

Lethbridge

I

N

Medicine Hat

Regina

S

N

UNITED STATES

PACIFIC OCEAN

0        250        500 kilometres

0        250        500

### Beaver

The American beaver is
the largest rodent in North
America. It can measure
1.35 metres from nose to tail.

Beavers build dams across rivers to form lakes, where they are safe fror
predators such as wolves and bears. Their dams are made from logs,
sticks and mud. Beavers then build homes in the lake, called lodges.

### Lakes and forests

There are thousands of freshwater lakes
and rivers in Canada, and almost half of the
country is covered in forest. Wood products,
especially wood pulp and paper, make up
a large part of Canada's export trade.

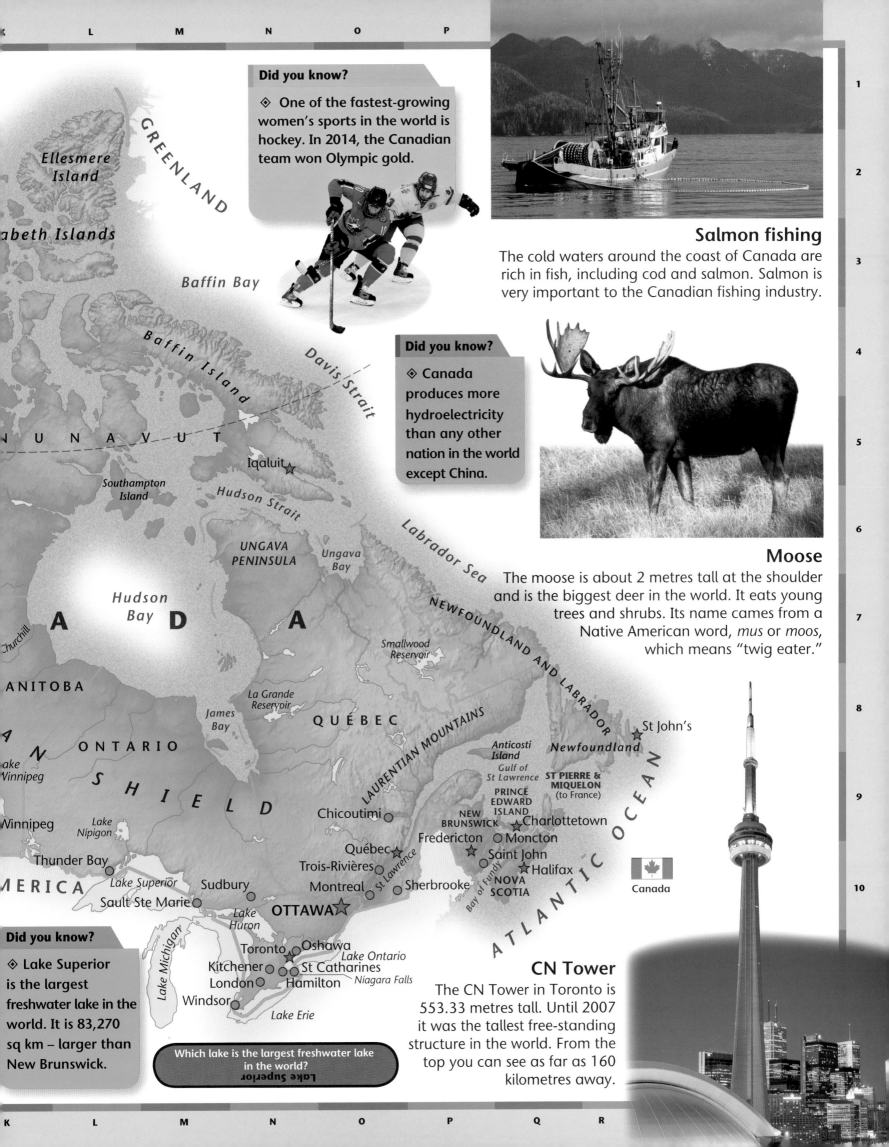

1
2
3
4
5
6
7
8
9
10

**Did you know?**

◈ One of the fastest-growing women's sports in the world is hockey. In 2014, the Canadian team won Olympic gold.

## Salmon fishing

The cold waters around the coast of Canada are rich in fish, including cod and salmon. Salmon is very important to the Canadian fishing industry.

**Did you know?**

◈ Canada produces more hydroelectricity than any other nation in the world except China.

## Moose

The moose is about 2 metres tall at the shoulder and is the biggest deer in the world. It eats young trees and shrubs. Its name came from a Native American word, *mus* or *moos*, which means "twig eater."

GREENLAND

Ellesmere Island

abeth Islands

Baffin Bay

Baffin Island

Davis Strait

N U N A V U T

Iqaluit ☆

Southampton Island

Hudson Strait

Churchill

Hudson Bay

A        D        A

UNGAVA PENINSULA

Ungava Bay

Labrador Sea

Smallwood Reservoir

NEWFOUNDLAND AND LABRADOR

ANITOBA

La Grande Reservoir

James Bay

Q U É B E C

LAURENTIAN MOUNTAINS

St John's ★

A N

ONTARIO

Anticosti Island

Newfoundland

ke Winnipeg

S H I E L D

Gulf of St Lawrence

ST PIERRE & MIQUELON (to France)

PRINCE EDWARD ISLAND

Chicoutimi ◯

NEW BRUNSWICK

Charlottetown ☆

Winnipeg

Lake Nipigon

Fredericton ◯ ◯ Moncton

Thunder Bay

Québec ☆
Trois-Rivières ◯

St Lawrence

☆ Saint John

☆ Halifax

MERICA

Lake Superior

Sudbury ◯

Montreal ◯ ◯ Sherbrooke

NOVA SCOTIA

Bay of Fundy

🇨🇦
Canada

Sault Ste Marie ◯

Lake Huron

OTTAWA ☆

ATLANTIC OCEAN

Toronto ◯ Oshawa
Kitchener ◯ ◯ St Catharines
London ◯ Hamilton
Windsor

Lake Michigan

Lake Ontario

Niagara Falls

Lake Erie

**Did you know?**

◈ Lake Superior is the largest freshwater lake in the world. It is 83,270 sq km – larger than New Brunswick.

Which lake is the largest freshwater lake in the world?
Lake Superior

## CN Tower

The CN Tower in Toronto is 553.33 metres tall. Until 2007 it was the tallest free-standing structure in the world. From the top you can see as far as 160 kilometres away.

# United States of America

NORTH AMERICA

**Country File**

United States of America

The United States of America (USA) covers an area almost the size of Europe. It includes the states of Alaska at the northwest tip of Canada, and Hawaii in the Pacific Ocean. The land and climate of the USA change dramatically across this huge area. There are deserts, mountains, prairies and swamps. In Alaska temperatures drop to below −30°C in winter. In the southeast the temperature rarely drops below 10°C. The population of over 318 million contains people descended from immigrants from all over the world, especially Europe. There are also 2.9 million Native American people. The USA is one of the world's wealthiest nations. There are huge oil and gas fields in Texas and Oklahoma, minerals are mined in Montana and Wyoming, and California is a centre for the computer industry.

Detroit has been home to the USA's motor industry since Henry Ford built his first vehicle there in 1896.

The sunny state of California produces half of the USA's fruit and vegetables.

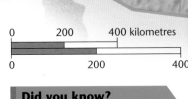

## Monument Valley

The great "buttes" of Monument Valley, on the border of Utah and Arizona, were formed by rivers, rain and wind, which have eroded the soft rock around them over millions of years. The land between the buttes was once as high as they are. Their red colour comes from iron oxide in the soil, which is also known as rust.

**Did you know?**

◇ The 10 highest mountains in the United States of America are all in Alaska. The highest is Mount McKinley.

**Did you know?**

◇ The Grand Canyon in Arizona is one of the natural wonders of the world.

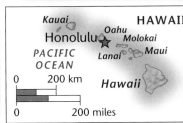

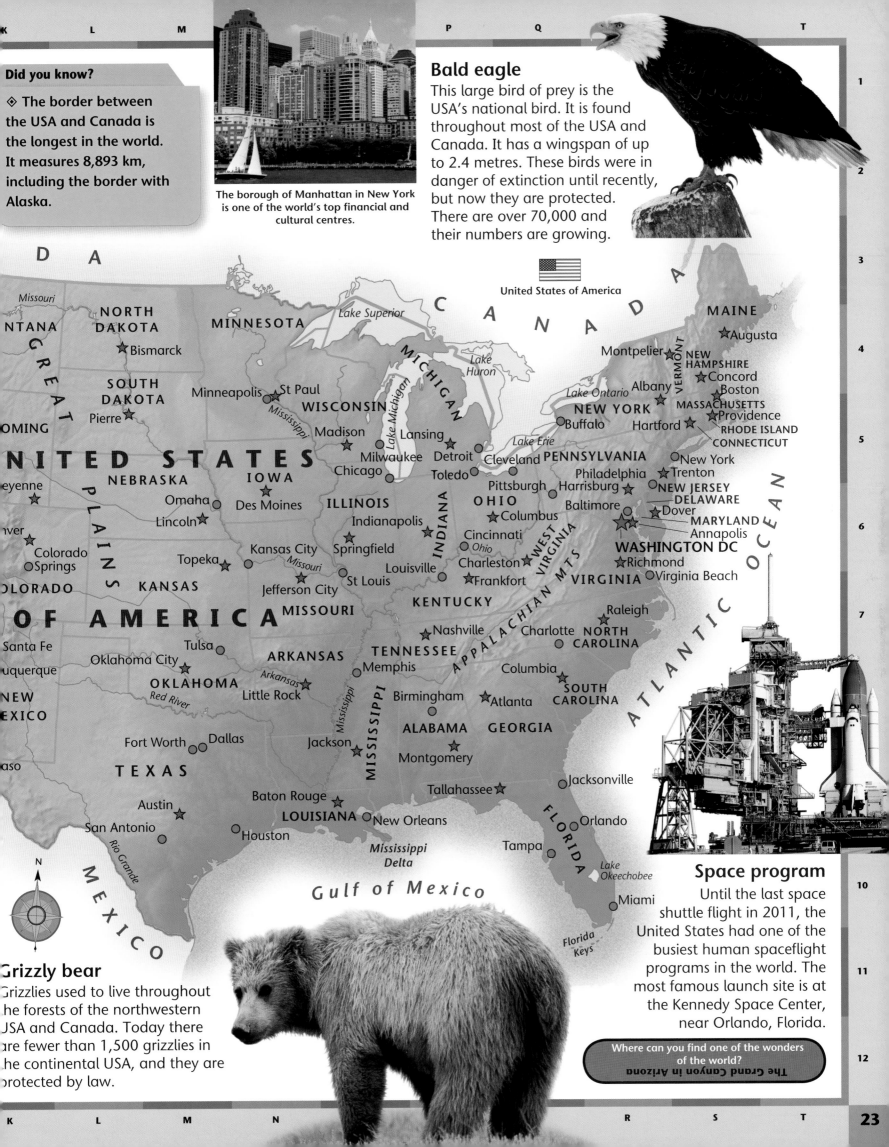

**Did you know?**

◈ The border between the USA and Canada is the longest in the world. It measures 8,893 km, including the border with Alaska.

The borough of Manhattan in New York is one of the world's top financial and cultural centres.

## Bald eagle

This large bird of prey is the USA's national bird. It is found throughout most of the USA and Canada. It has a wingspan of up to 2.4 metres. These birds were in danger of extinction until recently, but now they are protected. There are over 70,000 and their numbers are growing.

United States of America

CANADA

Missouri

NORTH DAKOTA
★ Bismarck

MINNESOTA
Lake Superior

MICHIGAN
Lake Huron

MAINE
★ Augusta

Montpelier
VERMONT
NEW HAMPSHIRE
★ Concord
Boston

NTANA

SOUTH DAKOTA
Minneapolis
St Paul
WISCONSIN
Madison
Lake Michigan
Lansing

Lake Ontario
Albany
NEW YORK
Buffalo
Hartford
MASSACHUSETTS
★ Providence
RHODE ISLAND
CONNECTICUT

OMING
Pierre
Mississippi

Milwaukee
Detroit
Chicago
Toledo
Lake Erie
Cleveland
PENNSYLVANIA
Philadelphia
Pittsburgh
Harrisburg
New York
★ Trenton
NEW JERSEY
DELAWARE

UNITED STATES

NEBRASKA
IOWA
ILLINOIS
INDIANA
OHIO
★ Columbus
Baltimore
★ Dover
MARYLAND

eyenne
Omaha
Des Moines
Indianapolis
Cincinnati
Ohio
Annapolis
WASHINGTON DC

Lincoln
Kansas City
Springfield
Louisville
Charleston
WEST VIRGINIA
Richmond
Virginia Beach

Colorado Springs
Topeka
Missouri
St Louis
Frankfort
VIRGINIA

nver

OLORADO
KANSAS
Jefferson City
KENTUCKY
APPALACHIAN MTS

OF AMERICA
MISSOURI
Nashville
Raleigh
Charlotte
NORTH CAROLINA

Santa Fe
Tulsa
ARKANSAS
TENNESSEE
Columbia
SOUTH CAROLINA

uquerque
Oklahoma City
Arkansas
Memphis
Birmingham
Atlanta

NEW
OKLAHOMA
Little Rock
Red River

EXICO
ALABAMA
GEORGIA
Montgomery

aso
Fort Worth
Dallas
Jackson
MISSISSIPPI

TEXAS
Mississippi
Jacksonville

Austin
Baton Rouge
Tallahassee

San Antonio
Houston
LOUISIANA
New Orleans
FLORIDA
Orlando

N

Mississippi Delta

Tampa
Lake Okeechobee

Gulf of Mexico
Miami

M E X I C O
Rio Grande

Florida Keys

ATLANTIC OCEAN

## Space program

Until the last space shuttle flight in 2011, the United States had one of the busiest human spaceflight programs in the world. The most famous launch site is at the Kennedy Space Center, near Orlando, Florida.

## Grizzly bear

Grizzlies used to live throughout the forests of the northwestern USA and Canada. Today there are fewer than 1,500 grizzlies in the continental USA, and they are protected by law.

Where can you find one of the wonders of the world?

The Grand Canyon in Arizona

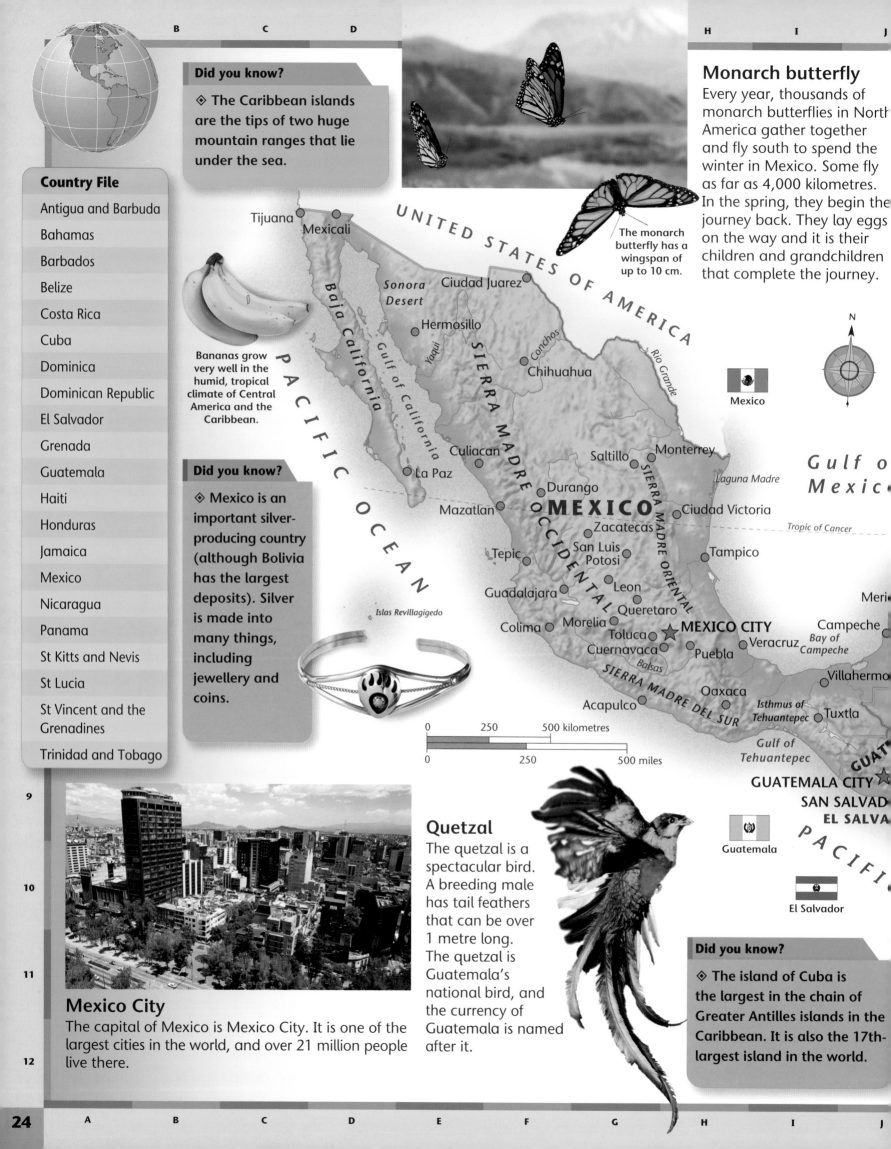

## Did you know?

◇ The Caribbean islands are the tips of two huge mountain ranges that lie under the sea.

## Did you know?

◇ Mexico is an important silver-producing country (although Bolivia has the largest deposits). Silver is made into many things, including jewellery and coins.

Bananas grow very well in the humid, tropical climate of Central America and the Caribbean.

## Monarch butterfly

Every year, thousands of monarch butterflies in North America gather together and fly south to spend the winter in Mexico. Some fly as far as 4,000 kilometres. In the spring, they begin the journey back. They lay eggs on the way and it is their children and grandchildren that complete the journey.

The monarch butterfly has a wingspan of up to 10 cm.

Mexico

## Mexico City

The capital of Mexico is Mexico City. It is one of the largest cities in the world, and over 21 million people live there.

## Quetzal

The quetzal is a spectacular bird. A breeding male has tail feathers that can be over 1 metre long. The quetzal is Guatemala's national bird, and the currency of Guatemala is named after it.

Guatemala

El Salvador

## Did you know?

◇ The island of Cuba is the largest in the chain of Greater Antilles islands in the Caribbean. It is also the 17th-largest island in the world.

### Map labels

Tijuana

Mexicali

UNITED STATES OF AMERICA

Sonora Desert

Ciudad Juarez

Baja California

Gulf of California

Hermosillo

Yaqui

Conchos

SIERRA MADRE OCCIDENTAL

Chihuahua

Rio Grande

PACIFIC OCEAN

Culiacan

Saltillo

Monterrey

Gulf of Mexico

Laguna Madre

La Paz

Durango

MEXICO

Ciudad Victoria

Mazatlan

Zacatecas

SIERRA MADRE ORIENTAL

Tropic of Cancer

Tepic

San Luis Potosi

Tampico

Islas Revillagigedo

Guadalajara

Leon

Colima

Morelia

Queretaro

MEXICO CITY

Meri

Toluca

Campeche

Cuernavaca

Veracruz

Bay of Campeche

Puebla

Balsas

Oaxaca

Villahermo

SIERRA MADRE DEL SUR

Acapulco

Isthmus of Tehuantepec

Tuxtla

Gulf of Tehuantepec

GUAT

GUATEMALA CITY

SAN SALVAD

EL SALVA

PACIFI

N

0    250    500 kilometres

0    250    500 miles

# Central America and the Caribbean

NORTH AMERICA

The continents of North and South America are linked by Central America. To the east are the Greater and Lesser Antilles islands, which are also known as the Caribbean islands. All along Central America there are mountains and volcanoes. In the north there are hot, dry deserts and in the south there are tropical rainforests. The Caribbean also has rainforests and a tropical climate. Most of the people who live in this region are descended from Africans, Asians and Europeans. In Central America, fishing, coffee and fruit-growing are important industries. Most of Mexico's income comes from oil and gas. Tourism and sugar farming are important in the Caribbean.

## Caribbean islands
The islands of the Caribbean are popular holiday destinations. Many tourists are attracted by the warm, clear sea, sandy beaches and tropical climate.

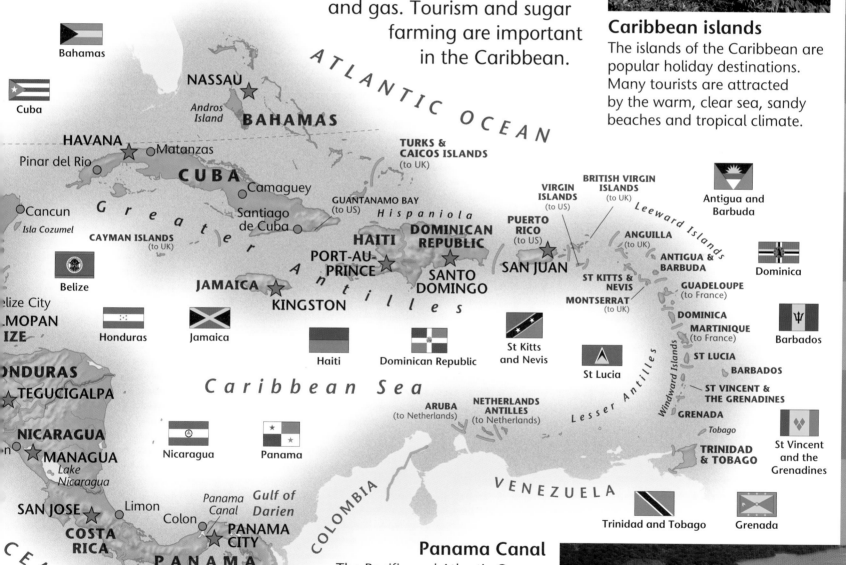

Bahamas

Cuba

NASSAU

Andros Island

BAHAMAS

ATLANTIC OCEAN

HAVANA
Matanzas
Pinar del Rio
CUBA
Camaguey
Cancun
Isla Cozumel
Greater
Santiago de Cuba
CAYMAN ISLANDS (to UK)

TURKS & CAICOS ISLANDS (to UK)

GUANTANAMO BAY (to US)

Hispaniola

Antilles

HAITI
DOMINICAN REPUBLIC
PORT-AU-PRINCE
SANTO DOMINGO
JAMAICA
KINGSTON

Belize

elize City
.MOPAN
IZE

Honduras

Jamaica

Haiti

Dominican Republic

St Kitts and Nevis

St Lucia

VIRGIN ISLANDS (to US)
BRITISH VIRGIN ISLANDS (to UK)
PUERTO RICO (to US)
SAN JUAN
ANGUILLA (to UK)
ANTIGUA & BARBUDA
ST KITTS & NEVIS
MONTSERRAT (to UK)
GUADELOUPE (to France)
DOMINICA
MARTINIQUE (to France)
ST LUCIA
BARBADOS
ST VINCENT & THE GRENADINES
GRENADA
Tobago

Leeward Islands

Antigua and Barbuda

Dominica

Barbados

Lesser Antilles

Windward Islands

Caribbean Sea

ARUBA (to Netherlands)
NETHERLANDS ANTILLES (to Netherlands)

ONDURAS
TEGUCIGALPA
NICARAGUA
MANAGUA
Lake Nicaragua

Nicaragua

Panama

St Vincent and the Grenadines

TRINIDAD & TOBAGO

VENEZUELA

COLOMBIA

SAN JOSE
Limon
COSTA RICA
Panama Canal
Colon
Gulf of Darien
PANAMA CITY
PANAMA

Trinidad and Tobago

Grenada

Costa Rica

OCEAN

## Panama Canal
The Pacific and Atlantic Oceans are linked by the Panama Canal. This waterway is about 80 kilometres long. By using the canal, a boat travelling from one coast of North America to the other can avoid going around Cape Horn in South America and cut its journey by about 15,000 kilometres.

Can you find the largest island in the Caribbean?
Cuba

# South America

SOUTH AMERICA

The continent of South America is home to the Amazon rainforest and mountains of the Andes. The Amazon River is about 6,500 kilometres long and is the greatest river in South America. The climate ranges from tropical in the north to bitterly cold in the south – the tip of South America is only 1,000 kilometres away from Antarctica. In between, the climate is less extreme. There are wide, open grasslands called the pampas, where cattle and cereals are farmed. Northern South America is rich in oil and gas, especially in Venezuela. Further south, copper and iron ore are found. Coffee is the most important crop in South America, and Brazil is the world's leading coffee grower. Cocoa, sugar cane and bananas are also important crops.

## Country File

- Argentina
- Bolivia
- Brazil
- Chile
- Colombia
- Ecuador
- Guyana
- Paraguay
- Peru
- Suriname
- Uruguay
- Venezuela

6

### Angel Falls

The highest waterfall in the world is Angel Falls in Venezuela. Angel Falls is almost 1 kilometre high – 19 times higher than Niagara Falls.

## Did you know?

◊ Bolivia has two capital cities – La Paz and Sucre. La Paz is 3,600 m above sea level, which makes it the highest capital city in the world.

◊ Ecuador exports more bananas than any other country in the world.

Many vegetables, such as tomatoes, potatoes, beans and corn, originally came from South America.

### Carnival time

Every year, just before Lent, Carnival begins in Rio de Janeiro, Brazil. For five days people dress up, dance and parade through the streets to the sound of samba music. There is a competition for the most outrageous costume and the best-decorated float.

10

## Amazon rainforest

The Amazon rainforest is the largest tropical rainforest in the world. Many scientists believe that more than one-third of all the world's species of plants and animals live there. About 16 square kilometres of Brazilian rainforest are destroyed every day, as the forest is cut down for timber and cleared for farming. If this continues, the rainforest will eventually be gone. Hundreds of thousands of species of animals and plants will be lost forever.

11

12

### Jaguar

For its size, the jaguar is one of the strongest mammals in the world. This cat can kill prey over three times its own body weight. It is good at climbing, crawling and swimming.

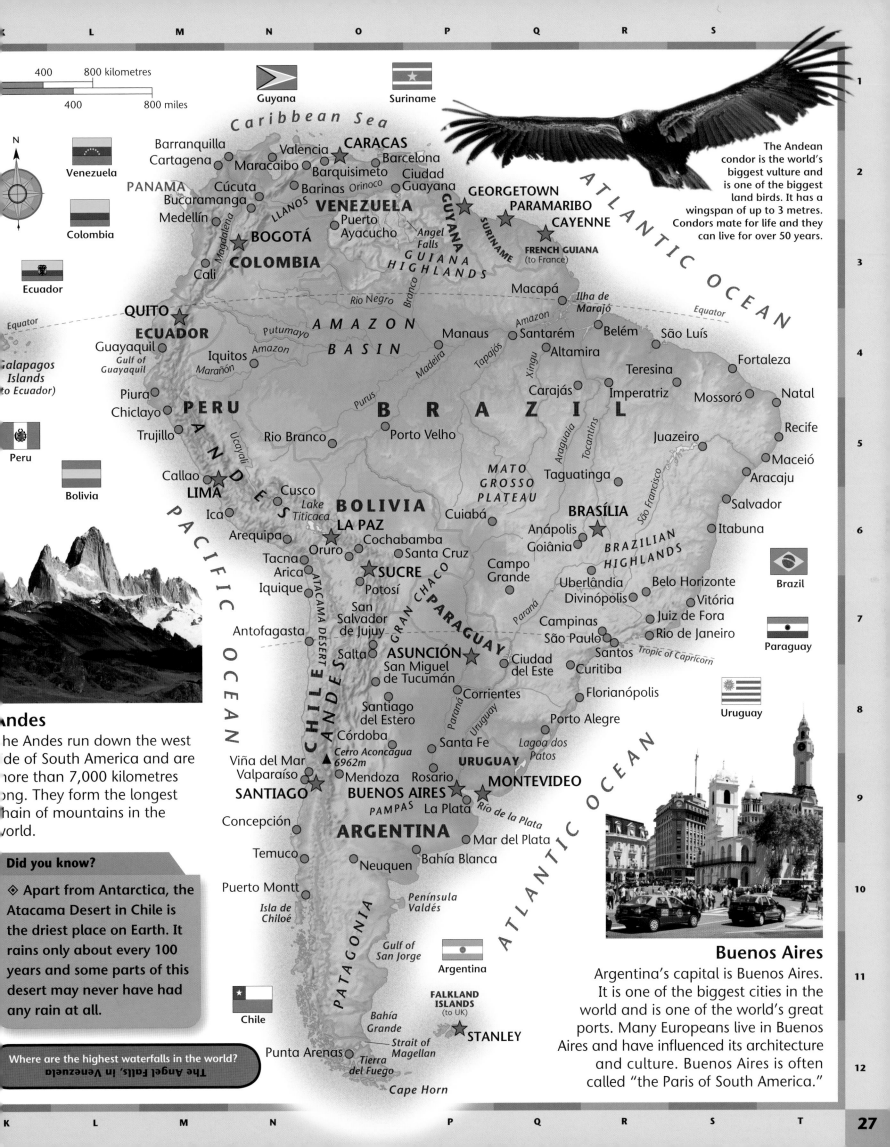

400    800 kilometres

400    800 miles

N

Guyana

Suriname

*Caribbean Sea*

**The Andean condor** is the world's biggest vulture and is one of the biggest land birds. It has a wingspan of up to 3 metres. Condors mate for life and they can live for over 50 years.

Venezuela

Colombia

Ecuador

Peru

Bolivia

Brazil

Uruguay

Argentina

Chile

PANAMA

Barranquilla
Cartagena
Cúcuta
Bucaramanga
Medellín
Cali

Valencia    CARACAS
Maracaibo    Barcelona
Barquisimeto
Barinas    Ciudad
Orinoco    Guayana

VENEZUELA
Puerto
Ayacucho

BOGOTÁ

COLOMBIA

GEORGETOWN
PARAMARIBO
CAYENNE

GUYANA
SURINAME

FRENCH GUIANA
(to France)

*Angel Falls*

*GUIANA HIGHLANDS*

*Magdalena*

*LLANOS*

*Branco*

*Rio Negro*

Macapá

*Ilha de Marajó*

*Equator*

*ATLANTIC OCEAN*

Equator

QUITO

ECUADOR
Guayaquil

*Gulf of Guayaquil*

*Galapagos Islands (to Ecuador)*

Iquitos

*Putumayo*

*Amazon*

*Marañón*

*AMAZON BASIN*

Manaus    Santarém    Belém    São Luís
Altamira
*Amazon*

*Madeira*    *Tapajós*    Teresina    Fortaleza

*Xingu*

Piura
Chiclayo
Trujillo

PERU

Rio Branco

Porto Velho

*Purus*

*Ucayali*

B R A Z I L

Carajás    Imperatriz    Mossoró    Natal

*Araguaia*    *Tocantins*

Juazeiro    Recife
Maceió
Aracaju

Callao
LIMA
Ica
Arequipa

Cusco

*Lake Titicaca*

BOLIVIA

LA PAZ
Cochabamba
Oruro    Santa Cruz

*MATO GROSSO PLATEAU*

Cuiabá

Taguatinga

BRASÍLIA

Anápolis
Goiânia

*BRAZILIAN HIGHLANDS*

Salvador
Itabuna

*São Francisco*

Tacna
Arica
Iquique

SUCRE
Potosí

*ATACAMA DESERT*

*GRAN CHACO*

Campo
Grande

Uberlândia
Divinópolis

Belo Horizonte
Vitória

Antofagasta

San
Salvador
de Jujuy

PARAGUAY

*Paraná*

Campinas
São Paulo

Juiz de Fora
Rio de Janeiro

Santos

*Tropic of Capricorn*

Salta

ASUNCIÓN

Ciudad
del Este

Curitiba

*PACIFIC OCEAN*

San Miguel
de Tucumán

Corrientes

Florianópolis

Santiago
del Estero

*Paraná*    *Uruguay*

Porto Alegre

Córdoba

*Cerro Aconcagua 6962m*

Viña del Mar
Valparaíso
SANTIAGO

Mendoza

Santa Fe

Rosario

*Lagoa dos Patos*

URUGUAY

MONTEVIDEO

*Río de la Plata*

BUENOS AIRES
La Plata

*PAMPAS*

Concepción

ARGENTINA

Mar del Plata

Temuco

Neuquen    Bahía Blanca

Puerto Montt

*Isla de Chiloé*

*Península Valdés*

*PATAGONIA*

*Gulf of San Jorge*

*CHILE   ANDES*

*ATLANTIC OCEAN*

FALKLAND
ISLANDS
(to UK)

*Bahía Grande*

STANLEY

*Strait of Magellan*

Punta Arenas    *Tierra del Fuego*

*Cape Horn*

## Andes

The Andes run down the west side of South America and are more than 7,000 kilometres long. They form the longest chain of mountains in the world.

### Did you know?

◇ Apart from Antarctica, the Atacama Desert in Chile is the driest place on Earth. It rains only about every 100 years and some parts of this desert may never have had any rain at all.

Where are the highest waterfalls in the world?
The Angel Falls, in Venezuela

## Buenos Aires

Argentina's capital is Buenos Aires. It is one of the biggest cities in the world and is one of the world's great ports. Many Europeans live in Buenos Aires and have influenced its architecture and culture. Buenos Aires is often called "the Paris of South America."

# Northern Africa

AFRICA

The continent of Africa is the second-largest in the world. Northern Africa is mostly covered by the Sahara, which is the world's largest hot desert. Few people live there because conditions are so harsh. Most people in Northern Africa live near the coast or along the River Nile. Crops such as dates, cork, grapes and olives are produced in the north of the region, and cocoa beans, peanuts and palm oil in the south. Textiles are made in every area, especially in the north, where rugs are produced. There are big deposits of oil and natural gas in Libya, and in countries such as Egypt, Tunisia and Morocco, tourism is important.

**Country File**

Algeria
Benin
Burkina Faso
Cameroon
Cape Verde
Central African Republic
Chad
Djibouti
Egypt
Eritrea
Ethiopia
Gambia
Ghana
Guinea
Guinea-Bissau
Ivory Coast
Liberia
Libya
Mali
Mauritania
Morocco
Niger
Nigeria
Senegal
Sierra Leone
Somalia
South Sudan
Sudan
Togo
Tunisia
Western Sahara

**Did you know?**

◇ Uranium, diamonds and gold are mined in northern Africa.

**Did you know?**

◇ Half of the world's cocoa beans are now grown in Northern Africa.

Tunisia

Algeria

Morocco

Western Sahara

Mauritania

Mali

Cape Verde

Senegal

Gambia

Guinea-Bissau

Guinea

Sierra Leone

Liberia

Ivory Coast

Burkina Faso

Ghana

Togo   Benin

Nigeria

*Mediter*

ALGIERS   TUN
Tanger   Oran   Constantine
RABAT   St
Casablanca
MOROCCO   TUNIS
Marrakech   ATLAS MOUNTAINS

ALGERIA

ATLANTIC OCEAN

LAAYOUNE

WESTERN SAHARA   Tropic of Cancer   AHAGGA

SAHARA

MAURITANIA

NOUAKCHOTT   MALI   NIGE

*Senegal*   Agadez

CAPE VERDE

S A H E

SENEGAL   *Niger*

PRAIA   DAKAR   NIAMEY

GAMBIA   BAMAKO

BANJUL   OUAGADOUGOU

BISSAU   BURKINA FASO

GUINEA-BISSAU   GUINEA   NIGER

CONAKRY   IVORY   BENIN   ABUJA

FREETOWN   COAST   TOGO

SIERRA LEONE   YAMOUSSOUKRO   GHANA   PORTO-NOVO

MONROVIA   Lagos

LIBERIA   Abidjan   ACCRA   LOME

Gulf of   Douala

Guinea   YAOUN

EQUATORIAL GUIN

**Fennec fox**
This desert mammal is sandy colour helps it to hide from prey. It keeps cool by losing body heat through its huge ears. This fox usually hunts at night when it is cooler.

0   400   800 kilometres

0   400   800 miles

12

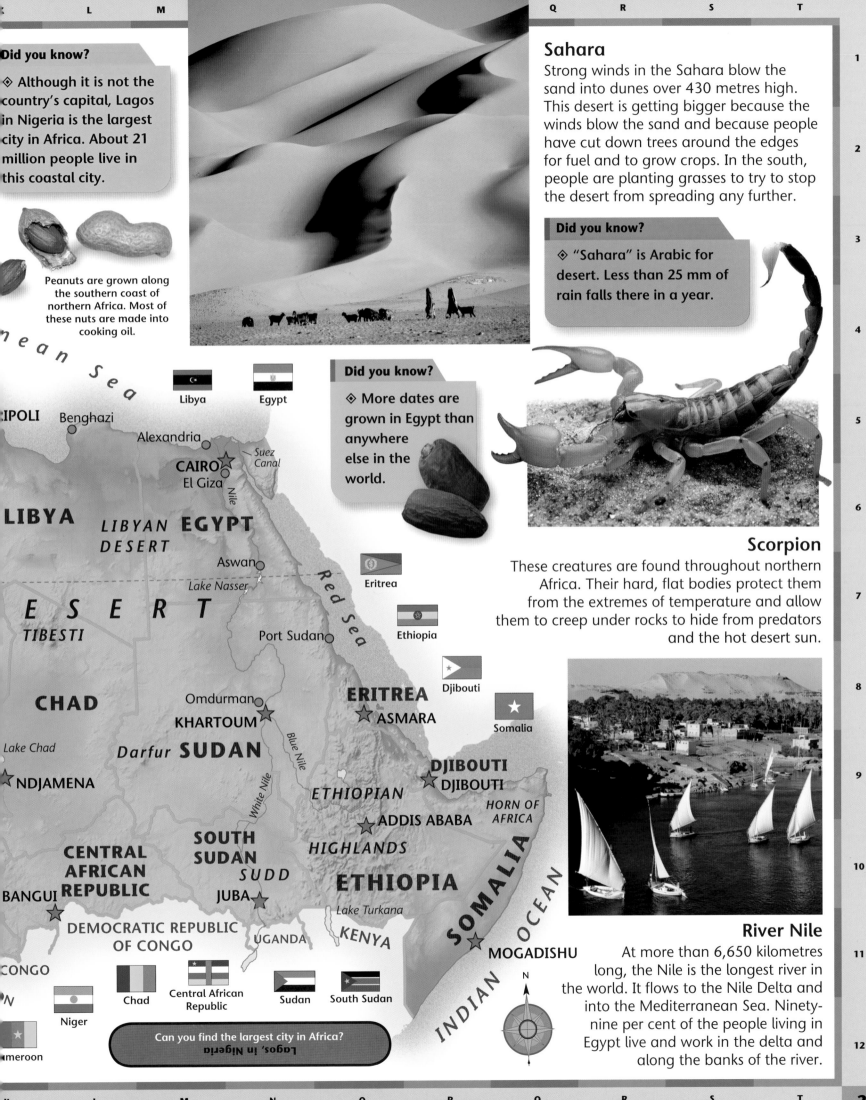

**Did you know?**

◇ Although it is not the country's capital, Lagos in Nigeria is the largest city in Africa. About 21 million people live in this coastal city.

Peanuts are grown along the southern coast of northern Africa. Most of these nuts are made into cooking oil.

## Sahara

Strong winds in the Sahara blow the sand into dunes over 430 metres high. This desert is getting bigger because the winds blow the sand and because people have cut down trees around the edges for fuel and to grow crops. In the south, people are planting grasses to try to stop the desert from spreading any further.

**Did you know?**

◇ "Sahara" is Arabic for desert. Less than 25 mm of rain falls there in a year.

**Did you know?**

◇ More dates are grown in Egypt than anywhere else in the world.

Libya

Egypt

*mean Sea*

IPOLI   Benghazi

Alexandria

CAIRO ☆   *Suez Canal*
El Giza
*Nile*

**LIBYA**   **LIBYAN DESERT**   **EGYPT**

Aswan
*Lake Nasser*

*Red Sea*

Eritrea

Ethiopia

Port Sudan

**E S E R T**

*TIBESTI*

**CHAD**   Omdurman
**KHARTOUM** ☆

Djibouti

Somalia

**ERITREA** ☆ **ASMARA**

*Lake Chad*   *Darfur* **SUDAN**
*Blue Nile*

☆ **NDJAMENA**

*White Nile*

**DJIBOUTI**
**DJIBOUTI**

*HORN OF AFRICA*

**CENTRAL AFRICAN REPUBLIC**

**SOUTH SUDAN**
*SUDD*

*ETHIOPIAN*

☆ **ADDIS ABABA**

*HIGHLANDS*

**ETHIOPIA**

**S O M A L I A**

*I N D I A N   O C E A N*

BANGUI ☆

JUBA ☆

*Lake Turkana*

**DEMOCRATIC REPUBLIC OF CONGO**   UGANDA   **KENYA**

☆ **MOGADISHU**

CONGO

'N

Niger

Chad   Central African Republic   Sudan   South Sudan

meroon

N

## Scorpion

These creatures are found throughout northern Africa. Their hard, flat bodies protect them from the extremes of temperature and allow them to creep under rocks to hide from predators and the hot desert sun.

## River Nile

At more than 6,650 kilometres long, the Nile is the longest river in the world. It flows to the Nile Delta and into the Mediterranean Sea. Ninety-nine per cent of the people living in Egypt live and work in the delta and along the banks of the river.

Can you find the largest city in Africa?
Lagos, in Nigeria

# Southern Africa

AFRICA

Southern Africa has many different climates. The Congo Basin is hot and humid and is the site of the world's second-biggest tropical rainforest. Further east and south are dry woodlands merging into savannah, which is a mixture of grassland and open woodland. It is there that the most well-known African animals are found. Further south is the Namib Desert, one of the hottest and driest places on Earth, with temperatures over 50°C during the day. Hundreds of different tribes live in southern Africa. There are hundreds of languages. The Kalahari Desert in Botswana is home to one of the few remaining groups of hunter-gatherers, the Bushmen, or San. In the 19th century, large gold and diamond deposits were found in South Africa, helping it to become the most powerful country in Southern Africa.

## Country File

Angola

Botswana

Burundi

Comoros

Congo

Democratic Republic of Congo

Equatorial Guinea

Gabon

Kenya

Lesotho

Madagascar

Malawi

Mauritius

Mozambique

Namibia

Rwanda

Sao Tome and Principe

Seychelles

South Africa

Swaziland

Tanzania

Uganda

Zambia

Zimbabwe

Many different crops are grown in Southern Africa, including citrus fruits and grapes, mainly for export

Congo

Equatorial Guinea

MALABO

EQUATORIAL GUINEA

CAMEROON

CENTRAL AF

SAO TOME

SAO TOME & PRINCIPE

LIBREVILLE

GABON

Mbandaka

Sao Tome and Principe

BRAZZAVILLE

KINSHA

CONGO

Congo

D

R

Gabon

ANGOLA

Kan

LUANDA

ANGOL

Angola

Huambo   BIÉ
PLATEAU

ATLANTIC

Namibe   Lubango

ANGOL

### Victoria Falls

This famous waterfall is on the Zambezi River, on the border between Zambia and Zimbabwe. It is 108 metres high and 1,708 metres wide. Local people call it "the smoke that thunders" because of the loud noise and spray that it makes.

OCEAN

NAMIBIA

WINDHO

KALA

NAMIB DESERT

DES

### Did you know?

◇ Diamonds are the world's hardest natural substance. Half of all the world's diamonds are mined in Southern Africa.

### African wildlife

Elephants, rhinoceroses, lions, leopards and buffalo are known as "the big five," and they attract thousands of tourists to Africa. Many are endangered species and they are protected by law.

Orange R

Namibia

Botswana

SO

CAPE TOWN

Cape of Good Hope

South Africa

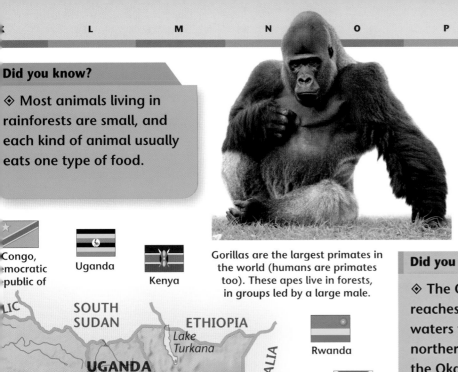

Congo, Democratic Republic of

Uganda

Kenya

Gorillas are the largest primates in the world (humans are primates too). These apes live in forests, in groups led by a large male.

## Kilimanjaro

The top of Kilimanjaro in Tanzania is covered in snow all year round, even though the mountain is close to the Equator. This is because the temperature drops as the land gets higher. Kilimanjaro is 5,895 metres high. It is the highest point in Africa.

Rwanda

Burundi

Tanzania

Seychelles

SOUTH SUDAN

ETHIOPIA
Lake Turkana

SOMALIA

UGANDA

KAMPALA

KENYA

Kisangani

Kisumu  Equator

Lake Victoria

RWANDA

KIGALI

NAIROBI

▲ Kilimanjaro 5895m

UMBURA  BURUNDI

Olduvai Gorge

Mombasa

Lake Tanganyika

SEYCHELLES

DODOMA

Zanzibar

ji-Mayi

Dar es Salaam

TANZANIA

GREAT RIFT VALLEY

Kolwezi

Comoros

Malawi

Lubumbashi

MALAWI

COMOROS

MORONI

Kitwe

Lake Nyasa

Ndola

LILONGWE

MAYOTTE
(to France)

Zambia

ZAMBIA

AKA

Zambezi

Blantyre

Mauritius

MADAGASCAR

HARARE

Mauritius
ANTANANARIVO

ZIMBABWE

Bulawayo

Beira

MOZAMBIQUE

MAURITIUS
PORT LOUIS

WANA

Limpopo

RÉUNION
(to France)

ORONE

Mozambique Channel

TSHWANE
(PRETORIA)

MBABANE

MAPUTO

Tropic of Capricorn

Johannesburg

SWAZILAND

EMFONTEIN

MASERU

Madagascar

N

Durban

Zimbabwe

THO

CA

AKENSBERG

INDIAN OCEAN

Mozambique

ort Elizabeth

Swaziland

esotho

## Baobab tree

The island of Madagascar, off the eastern coast of Africa, split off from the mainland millions of years ago. Many unique and unusual species of plants and animals developed there. Several types of baobab tree grow only in Madagascar. Some of these extraordinary trees are over 3,000 years old.

South Africa's climate is varied and is suitable for growing many types of cut flower, such as gerberas, roses and carnations. These are all exported to Europe, as well as being sold locally.

Which is the highest mountain in Africa?
Kilimanjaro, in Tanzania

0        400        800 kilometres

0        400        800 miles

# Northern Europe

EUROPE

Norway, Sweden and Denmark are known as Scandinavia. The countries of Estonia, Latvia and Lithuania are called the Baltic States. These six countries, together with Finland and Iceland, are the most northern in Europe. Most people in Scandinavia live in the cities or towns in the south and around the coast. Throughout Scandinavia there are forests, and many of the trees are used to make furniture and paper. Iron ore is used for making steel, and the water from the lakes and rivers is used to produce hydroelectricity. There are plenty of fish in the coastal waters of northern Europe, and all these countries have strong fishing industries.

## Country File

Denmark

Estonia

Finland

Iceland

Latvia

Lithuania

Norway

Sweden

## Lapland

The northern part of Norway, Sweden and Finland is known as Lapland. This is the home of the Sami people. Some Sami still herd reindeer, which they keep for their milk, meat and skins.

## Red squirrel

The red squirrel lives all over northern Europe. Although it is called "red" it can be black, brown or red with a pale belly. Other mammals, such as brown bears, elk and grey wolves, are also found in the forests of Scandinavia.

### Did you know?

◈ Finland has more than 188,000 lakes, and three-quarters of the country is covered by forest.

◈ Denmark has some of the longest beaches in Europe.

### Did you know?

◈ Iceland was rated the world's most peaceful country on the 2014 Global Peace Index.

Two-thirds of the land in Denmark is used for farming. Most of it is used for pig farming or for growing food for the pigs.

## Timber for building

Wood is a very important material for all of the countries in northern Europe. Over the centuries wood has been used for producing fuel, for making furniture and toys, and for building houses and churches. There are so many trees in this area that many houses and public buildings are still made from wood today.

## Norwegian fjords

Fjords are long, deep, steep-sided valleys, which glaciers carved through the mountains over 150,000 years ago. As the ice melted, the sea levels rose and the valleys flooded with water. Thousands of tourists visit the fjords each year to enjoy the beautiful scenery

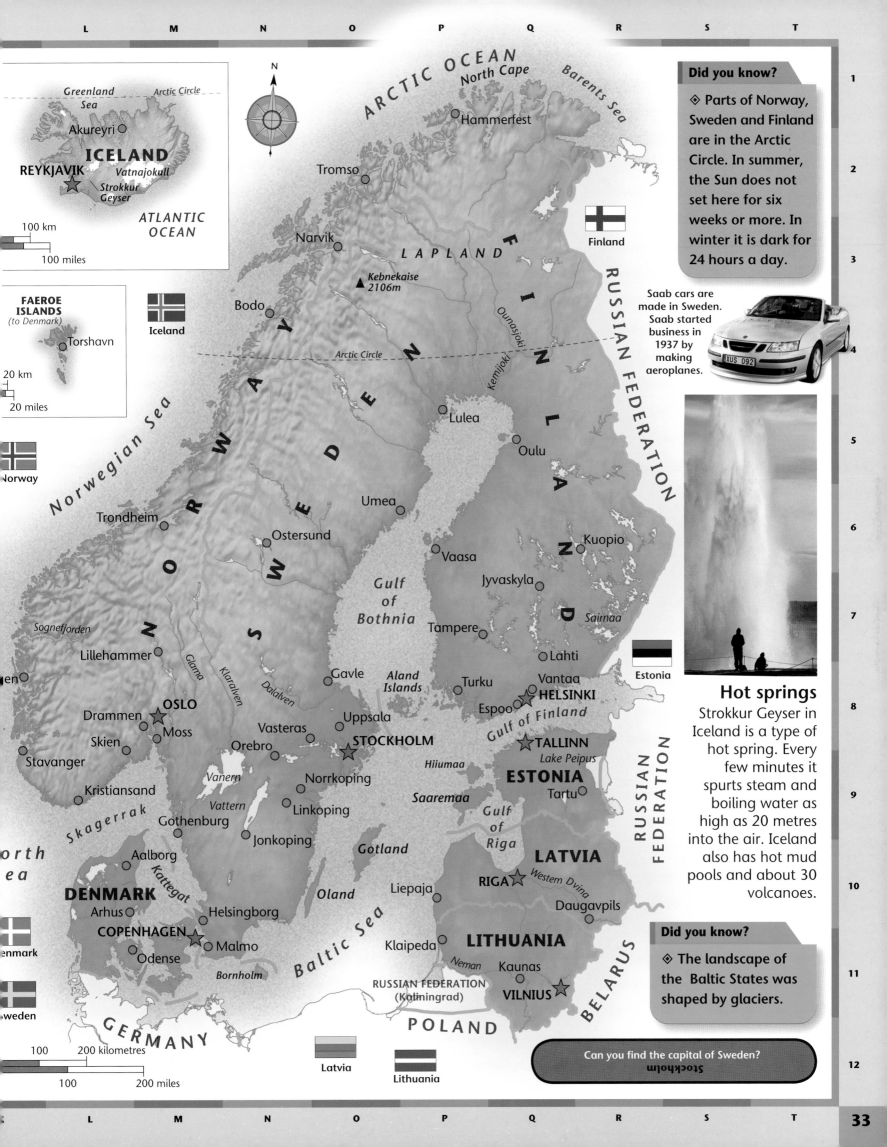

ARCTIC OCEAN

North Cape

Barents Sea

Hammerfest

### Did you know?

◈ Parts of Norway, Sweden and Finland are in the Arctic Circle. In summer, the Sun does not set here for six weeks or more. In winter it is dark for 24 hours a day.

Greenland Sea

Arctic Circle

Akureyri

## ICELAND
Vatnajokull
**REYKJAVIK**
Strokkur Geyser

ATLANTIC OCEAN

100 km
100 miles

N

Tromso

LAPLAND

Finland

Narvik

Kebnekaise
2106m

Bodo

Ounasjoki

Arctic Circle

Kemijoki

RUSSIAN FEDERATION

Saab cars are made in Sweden. Saab started business in 1937 by making aeroplanes.

XUS 092

### FAEROE ISLANDS
(to Denmark)

Torshavn

20 km
20 miles

Iceland

Lulea

Oulu

N
O
R
W
A
Y

S
W
E
D
E
N

F
I
N
L
A
N
D

Norwegian Sea

Norway

Trondheim

Ostersund

Umea

Vaasa

Kuopio

Jyvaskyla

Saimaa

Gulf
of
Bothnia

Tampere

Estonia

Sognefjorden

Lillehammer

Glomma

Klaralven

Dalalven

Gavle

Aland
Islands

Turku

Lahti

Vantaa

**HELSINKI**

Espoo

Gulf of Finland

en

**OSLO**

Drammen

Moss

Skien

Stavanger

Vasteras

Uppsala

**STOCKHOLM**

Hiiumaa

**TALLINN**
Lake Peipus

**ESTONIA**
Tartu

Hot springs

Strokkur Geyser in Iceland is a type of hot spring. Every few minutes it spurts steam and boiling water as high as 20 metres into the air. Iceland also has hot mud pools and about 30 volcanoes.

Kristiansand

Vanern

Norrkoping

Saaremaa

Gulf
of
Riga

Vattern

Linkoping

Skagerrak

Gothenburg

Jonkoping

Gotland

**LATVIA**

R
U
S
S
I
A
N

F
E
D
E
R
A
T
I
O
N

orth
ea

Aalborg

Kattegat

Oland

Liepaja

**RIGA**
Western Dvina

Daugavpils

## DENMARK
Arhus

Helsingborg

Baltic Sea

Klaipeda

**LITHUANIA**

### Did you know?

◈ The landscape of the Baltic States was shaped by glaciers.

enmark

**COPENHAGEN**
Odense
Malmo

Bornholm

Neman

Kaunas

**VILNIUS**

BELARUS

weden

100   200 kilometres
100   200 miles

G E R M A N Y

Latvia

Lithuania

RUSSIAN FEDERATION
(Kaliningrad)

P O L A N D

Can you find the capital of Sweden?
Stockholm

# Western Europe
EUROPE

The area in Europe that is furthest from Asia is known as western Europe. The most northern countries have a mild, wet climate. Further south the climate becomes increasingly warm. In southern France, Spain and Portugal, the temperature in summer often reaches over 30°C. The land is suitable for many kinds of farming. Oranges are grown in Spain, flowers in the Netherlands, and wheat and potatoes throughout western Europe. Many countries also grow grapes to make wine. Wine-making is important in France, Spain and Portugal. Most people in western Europe live in large towns and cities. Tourism is a big industry. Electronics and car manufacturing are also major industries in western Europe.

## Country File

Andorra

Belgium

France

Ireland

Luxembourg

Monaco

Netherlands

Portugal

Spain

United Kingdom

## Red fox

Foxes are members of the dog family. They are found all across Europe and survive in towns and cities as well as the countryside. They eat all kinds of things, such as worms, berries, insects, small mammals and household waste.

### Did you know?

◇ Only 26 land mammal species are native to Ireland.

One of the fastest trains i Europe is the French TGV *Train à Grande Vitesse*, which travels at a top speed of 300–320 km per hour. One TGV reached 574.8 km pe hour during a test run, whi is a world record for a trai travelling on ordinary rail

### Did you know?

◇ People from South America, Indonesia and the Caribbean make up five per cent of the population of the Netherlands. There used to be Dutch colonies in these places.

## Costa Brava

The coastal region in northeast Spain known as the Costa Brava stretches for about 160 kilometres along the Mediterranean Sea. It is popular for its sandy beaches and its warm seas. The area is also an important cork-growing region and supplies cork to wine producers all over the world.

Over 500 different varieties of cheese are made in France, including brie and roquefort.

## London Eye

Millions of tourists visit London every year for its history, theatres and sights, such as Big Ben and the London Eye. The London Eye is the world's fourth-tallest Ferris wheel, at 135 metres high. About 3.5 million people visit it each year to see the view from the top. Passengers can see for 40 kilometres in all directions.

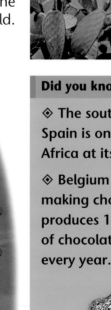

### Did you know?

◇ The southern tip of Spain is only 13 km from Africa at its closest point.

◇ Belgium is famous for making chocolate and produces 172,000 tonnes of chocolates every year.

Grapes grow on plants called vines, and the areas where wine is produced are called vineyards.

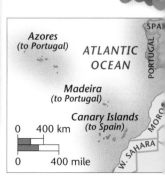

Azores (to Portugal)

ATLANTIC OCEAN

SPA

PORTUGAL

Madeira (to Portugal)

Canary Islands (to Spain)

0    400 km

0    400 mile

W. SAHARA

MORO

Shetland
Islands

Orkney
Islands

Outer
Hebrides

Inverness

Aberdeen

SCOTLAND

Dundee

Glasgow    Edinburgh

NORTHERN
IRELAND
Belfast

UNITED
KINGDOM

Newcastle
upon Tyne

Belgium    Netherlands

## Tulip fields

The Netherlands is famous
for its flower bulbs. It
produces 9 billion bulbs
every year. In spring the
Dutch tulip fields near
Amsterdam are ablaze
with colour. Visitors come
from all over the world
to see them.

Ireland

Galway   DUBLIN
IRELAND

Manchester    Leeds

Liverpool    Sheffield

N

Limerick

ENGLAND
Birmingham

North
Sea

Groningen

NETHERLANDS

THE    AMSTERDAM
HAGUE    Utrecht

GERMANY

WALES

Cork

A T L A N T I C

LONDON

Cardiff    Thames

Bristol

Rotterdam    Eindhoven

Ghent    Antwerp

Lille    BRUSSELS

BELGIUM

United Kingdom

Southampton

Plymouth    English Channel

Amiens    LUXEMBOURG

LUXEMBOURG

CHANNEL ISLANDS
(to UK)

Le Havre

Reims

Seine

Brest

O C E A N

PARIS
Strasbourg

Rennes

Meuse

Rhine

Orléans

Dijon

Luxembourg

Loire

SWITZERLAND

France

Nantes

F R A N C E

## Hedgehog

This small mammal lives
in many parts of Europe.
It has thousands of
short spines over
its back. If danger
threatens, it rolls itself
into a prickly ball.

Clermont-
Ferrand

Mt Blanc
4810m

Limoges

Lyon  A L P S

ITALY

Bay of
Biscay

Bordeaux    Dordogne

St-Étienne    Grenoble

MASSIF
CENTRAL

Rhône

Caronne

Nice

A Coruña    Gijón   Santander

Montpellier    MONACO

Toulouse

Marseille

Monaco

Oviedo

Bilbao

Vigo

Vitoria-Gasteiz

P Y R E N E E S

Perpignan

Corsica

Ajaccio

Viana do Castelo    Braga

Valladolid

Ebro

ANDORRA

Oporto

Duero

Zaragoza

Lleida

Costa Brava

Spain

SPAIN

Barcelona

Mediterranean  Sea

Coimbra

## Eiffel Tower

PORTUGAL

MADRID

This famous European
landmark is in Paris,
France. The Eiffel Tower is
324 metres high, including the
TV antenna on top. It is made
almost entirely of wrought iron.

Majorca    Minorca

LISBON

Toledo    Valencia

Palma

Mérida    Guadiana

Ibiza

Tagus

Albacete

Balearic Islands

Portugal

Guadalquivir

Alicante

Seville    Córdoba    Murcia

Andorra

Faro    Granada

Málaga

Gibraltar (to UK)

AFRICA

Which area is the largest producer of cork in the world?
Costa Brava, in Spain

# Central Europe

EUROPE

## Country File

Austria

Czech Republic

Germany

Italy

Liechtenstein

Malta

Poland

San Marino

Slovakia

Slovenia

Switzerland

Vatican City

The central part of Europe stretches from the Baltic Sea in the north to the Mediterranean Sea in the south. Winters can be very cold in the north, but the weather gets warmer the farther south you go. In Germany and Poland, land is used for mining, industry and farming. People grow crops such as potatoes and barley, and many farmers keep pigs and goats. Farther south, especially in Italy, people grow olives, grapes and citrus fruit. Many long rivers run through central Europe, including the Rhine and the Danube. People use these rivers for transporting their goods. A high mountain range called the Alps runs through France, Switzerland, Austria and northern Italy.

### Alps

This range of mountains is mainly in France, Italy, Switzerland and Austria and is about 1,200 kilometres long. Many people visit the Alps to climb, walk and ski.

### Did you know?

◈ Brown coal (lignite) is central Europe's main fuel and Germany is the world's largest producer. It contains lots of sulphur, and burning it to make electricity adds to air pollution and acid rain.

Lamborghini cars are made in Italy. They are some of the fastest, most expensive sports cars in the world.

### Did you know?

◈ Germany produces enough milk for its whole population.

### Vatican City

The Vatican City is in Rome, Italy. It is the smallest country in the world and it takes up an area of only 440,000 square metres. It contains St Peter's Basilica and the Apostolic Palace, where the Pope lives.

Tomatoes and basil are important ingredients in many Italian dishes.

### Alpine ibex

The ibex is a type of wild goat. It lives high up in the Alps and is sturdy and surefooted. The ibex was hunted almost to extinction in the 19th century, but now its numbers are growing.

### National parks

There are many national parks in central Europe. This is Triglav National Park in Slovenia. It contains Triglav mountain, which is the highest peak in Slovenia. There are beech and spruce forests, and animals such as chamois and lynx live here.

### Did you know?

◈ Pizza and pasta are traditional Italian foods, but they are now enjoyed all over the world.

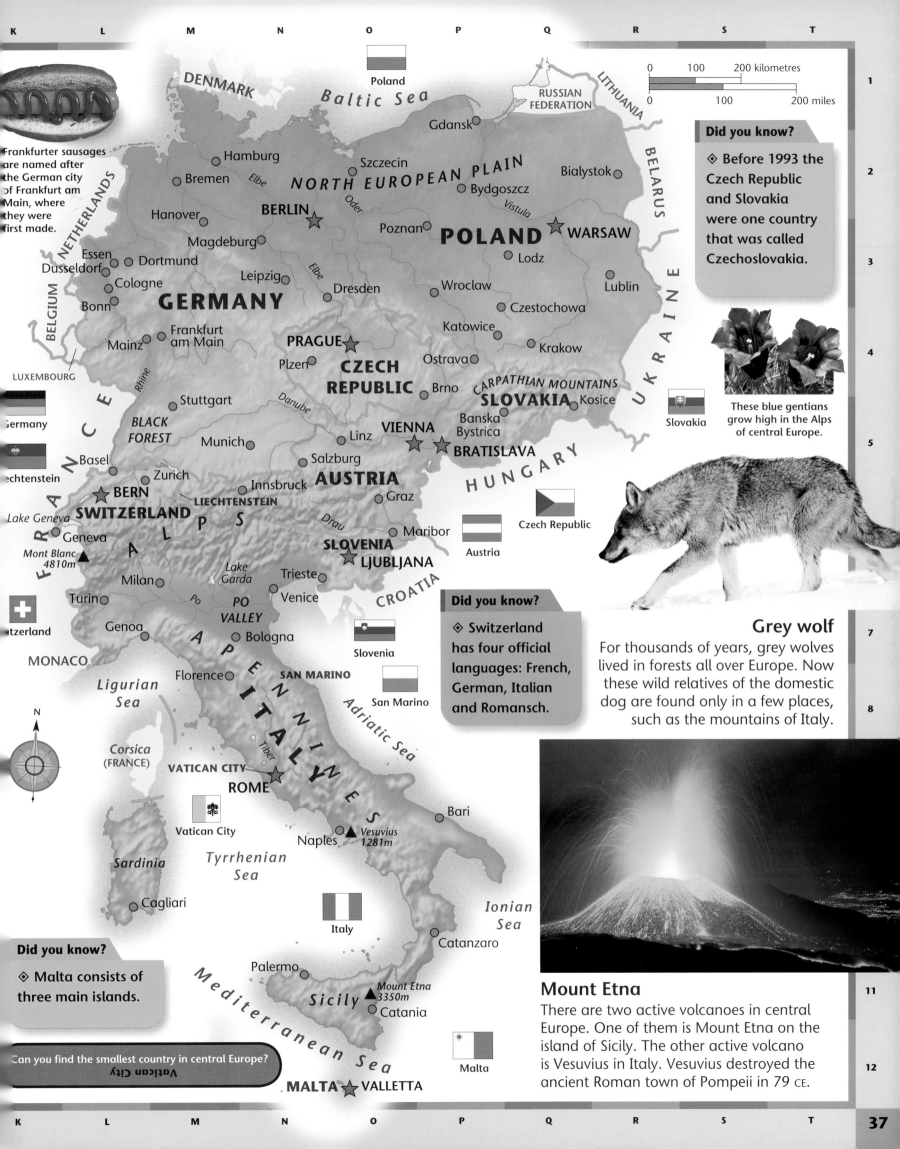

Frankfurter sausages are named after the German city of Frankfurt am Main, where they were first made.

**DENMARK**

*Baltic Sea*

**RUSSIAN FEDERATION**

LITHUANIA

Poland

Gdansk

Hamburg

Szczecin

Bialystok

BELARUS

Bremen

NORTH EUROPEAN PLAIN

Bydgoszcz

*Elbe*

Hanover

**BERLIN**

*Oder*

Poznan

**POLAND**

☆ **WARSAW**

*Vistula*

Magdeburg

Lodz

NETHERLANDS

Essen

Dortmund

Leipzig

Dresden

Wroclaw

Lublin

Dusseldorf

Cologne

**GERMANY**

Czestochowa

BELGIUM

Bonn

Frankfurt am Main

Katowice

Krakow

UKRAINE

Mainz

*Rhine*

**PRAGUE** ☆

Ostrava

LUXEMBOURG

Plzen

**CZECH REPUBLIC**

Brno

CARPATHIAN MOUNTAINS

Stuttgart

*Danube*

**SLOVAKIA**

Kosice

FRANCE

BLACK FOREST

Munich

Linz

**VIENNA** ☆

Banska Bystrica

Germany

Basel

Zurich

Salzburg

☆ **BRATISLAVA**

echtenstein

**BERN** ☆

Innsbruck

**AUSTRIA**

HUNGARY

LIECHTENSTEIN

*Lake Geneva*

**SWITZERLAND**

Graz

Slovakia

witzerland

Geneva

ALPS

*Drau*

Maribor

*Mont Blanc 4810m* ▲

**SLOVENIA** ☆ **LJUBLJANA**

Austria

Milan

*Lake Garda*

Trieste

CROATIA

Turin

*Po*

**PO VALLEY**

Venice

MONACO

Genoa

Bologna

Slovenia

APENNINES

Florence

**SAN MARINO**

*Ligurian Sea*

ITALY

San Marino

Czech Republic

**Grey wolf**

For thousands of years, grey wolves lived in forests all over Europe. Now these wild relatives of the domestic dog are found only in a few places, such as the mountains of Italy.

**Did you know?**

◇ Before 1993 the Czech Republic and Slovakia were one country that was called Czechoslovakia.

**Did you know?**

◇ Switzerland has four official languages: French, German, Italian and Romansch.

N

*Corsica (FRANCE)*

**VATICAN CITY** ☆

**ROME**

Vatican City

*Adriatic Sea*

*Tiber*

*Tyrrhenian Sea*

Bari

Naples

*Vesuvius 1281m* ▲

*Sardinia*

*Ionian Sea*

Cagliari

Italy

Catanzaro

**Did you know?**

◇ Malta consists of three main islands.

Palermo

*Mediterranean Sea*

*Sicily*

*Mount Etna 3350m* ▲

Catania

Malta

**MALTA** ☆ **VALLETTA**

**Mount Etna**

There are two active volcanoes in central Europe. One of them is Mount Etna on the island of Sicily. The other active volcano is Vesuvius in Italy. Vesuvius destroyed the ancient Roman town of Pompeii in 79 CE.

Can you find the smallest country in central Europe?

Vatican City

0 100 200 kilometres
0 100 200 miles

# Southeast Europe
EUROPE

Much of this area is mountainous, although there are fertile, flat areas in the north and east. Farming is important in these countries and many crops, such as grapes, tobacco, roses and wheat, are grown. In the north, the winters are very cold. Further south and around the coast, winters are milder and summers are hot and dry. During the past 30 years there have been many changes and wars in southeast Europe, caused by political, ethnic and religious problems. In the 1990s, Ukraine, Belarus and Moldova gained independence from the former Soviet Union. The former Yugoslavia split into the republics of Croatia, Serbia, Bosnia and Herzegovina, Macedonia and Montenegro. After years of war, some areas are still recovering from their problems.

## Country File

- Albania
- Belarus
- Bosnia and Herzegovina
- Bulgaria
- Croatia
- Greece
- Hungary
- Macedonia
- Moldova
- Montenegro
- Romania
- Serbia
- Ukraine

Most of the world's rose oil is produced in Bulgaria. Rose oil is used in luxury perfumes, soaps and cosmetics.

**Did you know?**

◈ Some of the water from the springs in Budapest is over 90°C. It has to be mixed with cold water before it can be used.

## Dubrovnik

The town of Dubrovnik in Croatia is encircled by 1,940 metres of city walls, which were built over 400 years ago. There are several towers and fortresses along the walls, making it one of the strongest fortifications in Europe.

**Did you know?**

◈ The European bison has been reintroduced to the Byelavyezhskaya forest in Belarus and Poland. It was extinct in the wild.

## Budapest

The Hungarian city of Budapest sits on a geological fault line. There are more than 120 springs in the city, where hot water rises naturally from the ground. People have built spas and baths over the hot springs for almost 2,000 years.

## Wild boar

There are wild boars roaming freely throughout the forests of southeast Europe. These nocturnal animals forage for food from dusk until dawn. They live in groups called sounders, containing about 20 animals. The groups are made up of three or four females and their young.

Olives have been grown in Greece for over 2,000 years, and olives and olive oil are major exports. Olives are also important ingredients in many dishes.

## Acropolis

Athens, the capital of Greece, is named after Athena, the goddess of war in Greek mythology. The Parthenon is Athena's chief temple. It was built in the 5th century BCE on the Acropolis hill above Athens. Acropolis means "edge of the city."

## Ukraine

The rich, dark soil of Ukraine is ideal for farming. Formerly part of the Soviet Union, Ukraine used to be known as "the bread basket of Russia." Today it exports large amounts of grain, vegetables, dairy products, meat and sunflower seeds.

Much of the soil in Moldova is rich and fertile. Many vegetables are grown there, but grapes and sunflowers are the most important crops.

Belarus

Ukraine

**LITHUANIA**

**LATVIA**

Vitsyebsk

**BELARUS**

**MINSK**

Mahilyow

Hrodna

**RUSSIAN FEDERATION**

Babruysk

Homyel'

Dnieper

Brest

*Pripet*

*Pripet Marshes*

Chernihiv

Chernobyl'

Luts'k

**KIEV**

Kharkiv

Zhytomyr

*Donets*

L'viv

**U K R A I N E**

Cherkasy

Poltava

Luhans'k

Ivano-Frankivs'k

Kirovohrad

*Dnieper*

Dnipropetrovs'k

**P O L A N D**

Chernivtsi

*Dniester*

Donets'k

**CARPATHIAN MOUNTAINS**

**MOLDOVA**

*Southern Bug*

Zaporizhzhya

Iasi

*Prut*

**CHISINAU**

Kryvyy Rih

Mariupol'

Bacau

Tiraspol'

Mykolayiv

**BLACK SEA LOWLAND**

*Sea of Azov*

Odesa

Bosnia and Herzegovina

Hungary

**AUSTRIA**

**SLOVAKIA**

Miskolc

*Tisza*

Nyiregyhaza

Gyor

**BUDAPEST**

Debrecen

**SLOVENIA**

Croatia

*Drava*

Pecs

Cluj-Napoca

**HUNGARY**

Szeged

*Transylvania*

**CRIMEA**
(annexed by Russia, disputed by Ukraine)

Moldova

**ZAGREB**

**CROATIA**

Osijek

*Sava*

Novi Sad

Timisoara

**ROMANIA**

Brasov

Galati

Simferopol'

Rijeka

Banja Luka

Tuzla

**TRANSYLVANIAN ALPS**

Ploiesti

Braila

*Black Sea*

Zadar

**BOSNIA & HERZEGOVINA**

**BELGRADE**

**BUCHAREST**

*Adriatic Sea*

**SARAJEVO**

**SERBIA**

Craiova

Ruse

*Dalmatia*

Split

*Danube*

Montana

Mostar

Nis

**BULGARIA**

Constanta

Romania

Dubrovnik

**MONTENEGRO**

**PRISTINA**

**BALKAN MOUNTAINS**

Varna

**PODGORICA**

**KOSOVO**

**SOFIA**

Serbia

Shkoder

**RHODOPE**

Sliven

Burgas

Bulgaria

(only partially recognized)

**SKOPJE**

Plovdiv

Durres

**MACEDONIA**

*Musala 2925m*

**MOUNTAINS**

Komotini

**TURKEY**

**TIRANA**

*Lake Ohrid*

Bitola

Kavala

*Lake Prespa*

Salonica

Montenegro

**ALBANIA**

Macedonia

Albania

Kerkyra

**PINDOS MOUNTAINS**

Larisa

*Aegean Sea*

*Corfu*

Arta

**GREECE**

*Lesbos*

*Sea*

**TURKEY**

Lamia

Greece

*Ionian Sea*

**ATHENS**

Patra

Piraeus

*Peloponnese*

*Cyclades*

*Dodecanese*

*Mediterranean Sea*

*Rhodes*

*Sea of Crete*

Irakleio

*Crete*

## Pine marten

These animals are related to weasels and are about the size of a domestic cat. They live in wooded areas all over Europe and spend a lot of their time in trees, where they build their dens. Pine martens feed mostly on small mammals, birds, frogs, insects and carrion.

N

| 0 | 100 | 200 kilometres |
|---|-----|----------------|
| 0 | 100 | 200 miles |

Can you find the city with lots of hot water springs?
Budapest, in Hungary

# Russian Federation

EUROPE AND ASIA

The Russian Federation is the largest country in the world. It stretches across two continents. The area to the west of the Ural Mountains is in Europe, and the area to the east is in Asia. Russia's climate varies massively, from Arctic weather in the north to mild weather in the south. More than three-quarters of the country is occupied by Siberia, but less than 30 per cent of the population lives there because the region has such long, cold winters. Siberia contains huge deposits of oil and natural gas. Russia also has fertile farmland and rich mineral deposits. Its main exports are oil and oil products, natural gas, metals, wood and wood products. Most of the people there are Russians, but there are more than 120 other ethnic groups with many different religions, languages and cultures.

**Country File**

Russian Federation

**Russian Federation**

**Franz Josef Land**

NORWAY
FINLAND
ESTONIA
LITH.
LATVIA
POLAND
KALININGRAD
(to Russia)
Kaliningrad
BELARUS
UKRAINE

Murmansk
KOLA PENINSULA
Arctic Circle
White Sea
Barents Sea
Novaya Zemlya
Kara Sea
Lake Ladoga
Petrozavodsk
St Petersburg
Lake Onega
Archangel
Velikiy Novgorod
Pechora
Northern Dvina
Vorkuta
YAMAL PENINSULA
Tver'
NORTH EUROPEAN PLAIN
Syktyvkar
Ob'
MOSCOW
Yaroslavl'
Tula
Ryazan'
Nizhniy Novgorod
Kirov
WEST SIBERIAN PLAIN
Don
CENTRAL RUSSIAN UPLAND
CRIMEA
(Annexed by Russia, disputed by Ukraine)
Voronezh
Kazan'
Izhevsk
Perm'
URAL MOUNTAINS
R U
Penza
Ul'yanovsk
Rostov-na-Donu
Saratov
Volga
Samara
Ufa
Yekaterinburg
Ob'
Volgograd
Tyumen
Krasnodar
Orenburg
Chelyabinsk
Trans-Siberian Railway
Irtysh
Stavropol'
El'brus 5642m
Astrakhan'
CAUCASUS
Groznyy
Caspian Sea
Omsk
Tomsk
GEORGIA
KAZAKHSTAN
Novosibirsk
Ob'
Keme
Barnaul
Novokuznets
AZERBAIJAN

## St Basil's Cathedral

St Basil's in Moscow is one of the most famous buildings in the world. It was built in Red Square by Tsar Ivan IV and was finished in 1560, after five years of building. It is actually eight separate churches, joined together with a central tower.

**Did you know?**

◇ Russia has two great classical ballet companies, called the Bolshoi and Mariinsky (formerly called the Kirov), which are both famous around the world.

## Siberian tiger

The Siberian tiger is in danger of extinction. Its habitat is being destroyed and it is hunted for its body parts, which are used in traditional Chinese medicine. There are only about 500 left in the wild.

## Reindeer

Herds of reindeer live on the tundra near the Arctic Circle. Herding reindeer is an important part of everyday life for many people in northern Russia. People depend on the animals for transport, food, clothing and shelter.

## Mineral reserves

This diamond mine in Mirny, Siberia, was once the world's biggest. Mining is a big part of Russia's economy and there are mines throughout the country. Other minerals include nickel, iron ore, copper, phosphates, cobalt and gold.

0    200    400 kilometres

0    200    400 miles

Severnaya Zemlya

New Siberian Islands

Laptev Sea

East Siberian Sea

Wrangel Island

Chukchi Sea

TAYMYR PENINSULA

NORTH SIBERIAN LOWLAND

Norilsk

CENTRAL SIBERIAN PLATEAU

Lena

VERKHOYANSKIY KHREBET

KHREBET CHERSKOGO

Indigirka

Kolyma

Arctic Circle

KOLYMA RANGE

KORYAK RANGE

Bering Sea

## Siberian crane

The Siberian crane is critically endangered. It lives in the wetlands of Siberia, which are gradually being destroyed for oil exploration and development.

S  I  B  E  R  I  A

Aldan

Yakutsk

Mirny

Lena

Magadan

Vulkan Klyuchevskaya Sopka 4750m

KAMCHATKA PENINSULA

Petropavlovsk-Kamchatskiy

Sea of Okhotsk

Angara

Krasnoyarsk

STANOVOY KHREBET

Sakhalin

Lake Baikal

YABLONOVYY KHREBET

Trans-Siberian Railway

Amur

Yenisey

Irkutsk

Ulan-Ude

Chita

Khabarovsk

CHINA

Kurile Islands

(Claimed by Japan)

PACIFIC OCEAN

### Did you know?

◈ Russian wooden dolls, which fit inside each other, are some of the most popular Russian souvenirs. These dolls were first made in 1890.

MONGOLIA

### Did you know?

◈ Russian cooking is famous for soups, including borscht, which is made from beets and cabbage.

Vladivostok

Sea of Japan

NORTH KOREA

JAPAN

Which region is more than three-quarters of Russia?
Siberia

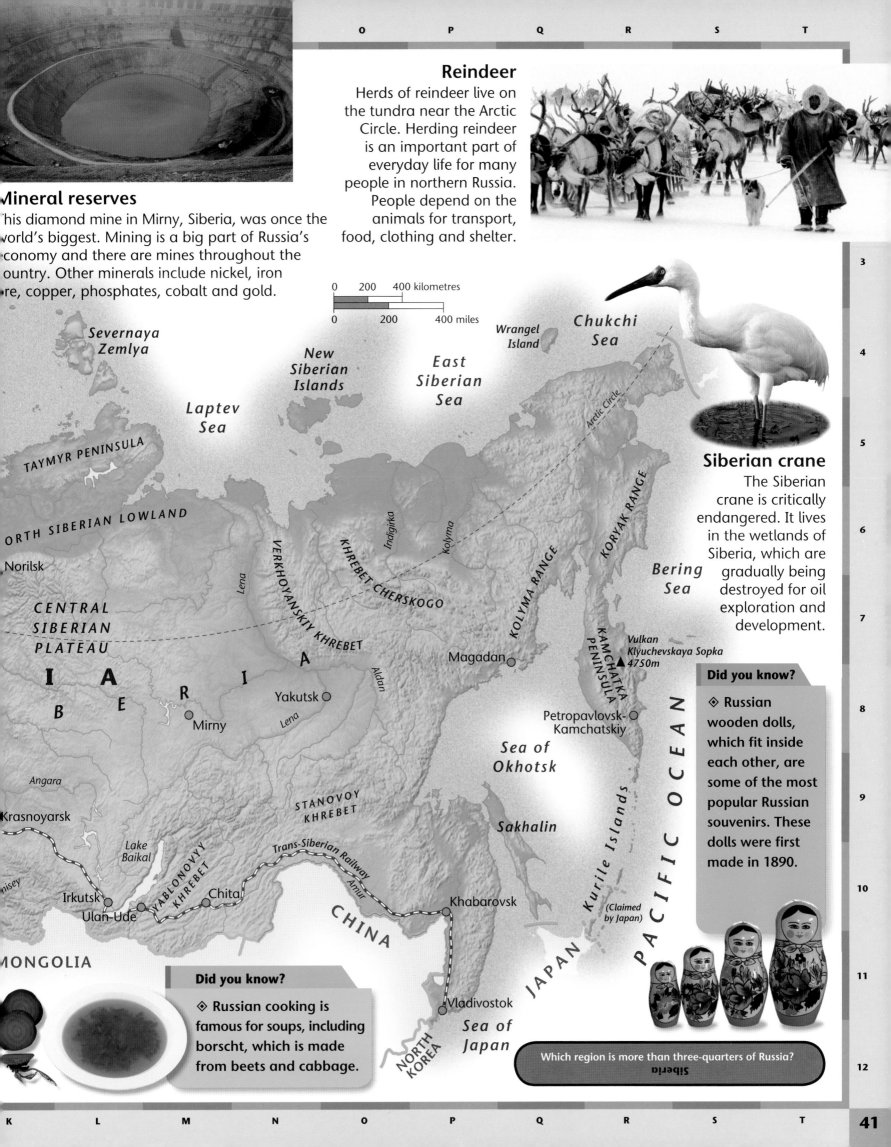

# Southwest Asia

ASIA

## Country File

- Armenia
- Azerbaijan
- Bahrain
- Cyprus
- Georgia
- Iran
- Iraq
- Israel
- Jordan
- Kuwait
- Lebanon
- Oman
- Qatar
- Saudi Arabia
- Syria
- Turkey
- United Arab Emirates
- Yemen

Almost all of Southwest Asia is desert. Temperatures can soar to over 30°C in the summer and very little rain falls. Although the weather is hot and dry, people have lived here, in cities and towns, for over 7,000 years. Three of the world's most important religions started here: Christianity, Islam and Judaism. This area has suffered wars for thousands of years and the conflicts still continue. The biggest source of income for many of these countries is from oil and gas. Tourism is an important industry in several countries, including Turkey and Israel. Turkey and Iran are famous for carpets, which are exported around the world.

Cyprus

BULGARIA

Istanb

Bur

GREECE

Izmir

Denizl

TURKISH REPUBLI
NORTHERN CYP
*(recognized only by Tu*

Syria

M e

Lebanon

### Mecca
The Ka'bah, a shrine inside the Sacred Mosque in Mecca in Saudi Arabia, is regarded by Muslims as the most sacred place on Earth.

Eggplants, apricots, pistachios and walnuts are important crops in this area.

### Petra
The ancient city of Petra, in Jordan, lies deep inside a desert gorge. Most of the buildings were carved out of solid rock. Once, this ruined city was the capital of an Arab kingdom. Now it is a popular tourist attraction.

### Did you know?
◈ Turkey is one of the few countries in the world that produces enough food for all its people. Half of the land in Turkey is used for agriculture (farming).

### Arabian oryx
The Arabian oryx was hunted to extinction in the wild. Then, after a worldwide breeding program in zoos, it was re-introduced into the wild in Oman. Today there are two herds of oryx roaming freely.

### Duba
The Burj al-Arab hotel in Dubai, in the United Arab Emirates, was the tallest hotel in the world when i opened in 1999. It is 321 metre high and has a helicopter pac on the 28th floor The hotel stand on an artificia island, and was designe to look like big sai

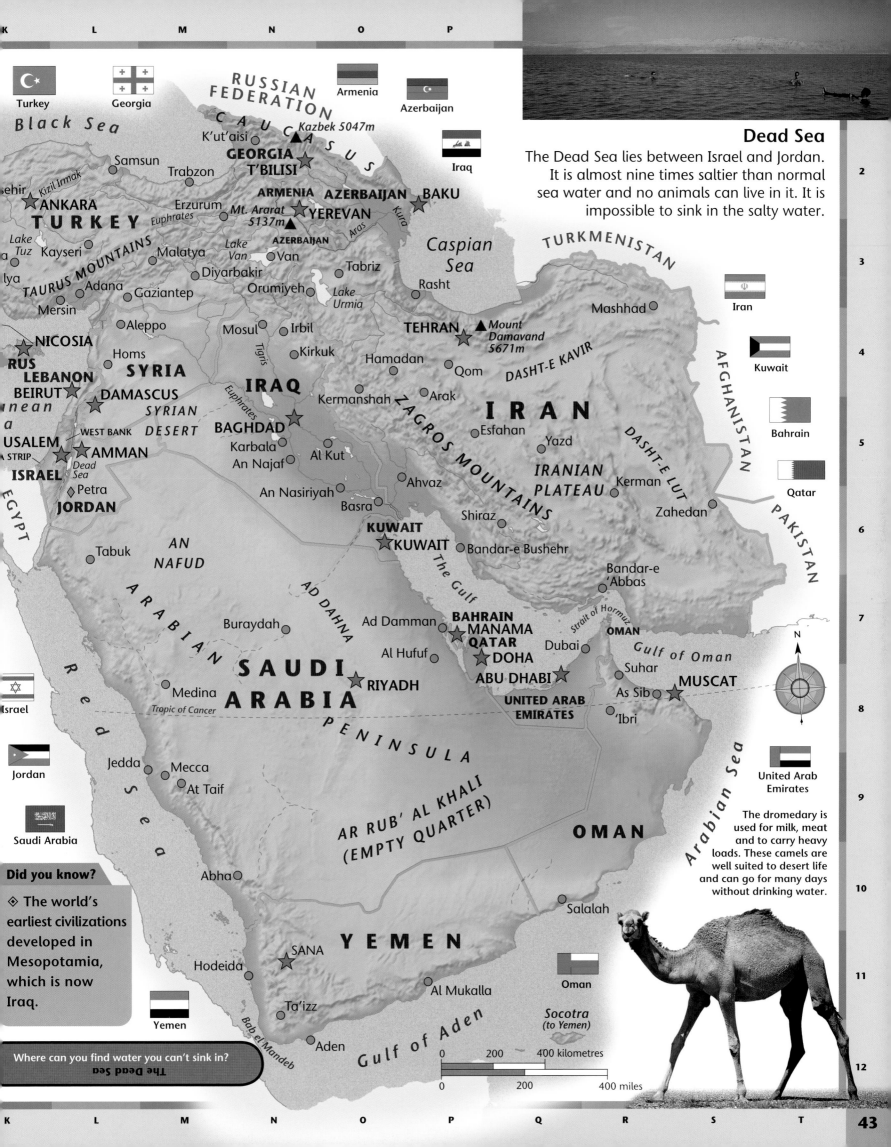

Turkey

Georgia

RUSSIAN FEDERATION

Armenia

Azerbaijan

Iraq

**Dead Sea**

The Dead Sea lies between Israel and Jordan. It is almost nine times saltier than normal sea water and no animals can live in it. It is impossible to sink in the salty water.

*Black Sea*

C A U C A S U S

Kazbek 5047m ▲

K'ut'aisi

Samsun

Trabzon

**GEORGIA**
**T'BILISI** ★

ehir    *Kizil Irmak*

★**ANKARA**

**T U R K E Y**

*Euphrates*

Erzurum

**ARMENIA**  **AZERBAIJAN**

★ **BAKU**

★ **YEREVAN**

Mt. Ararat
5137m▲

*Kura*

**AZERBAIJAN**

*Aras*

*Caspian
Sea*

TURKMENISTAN

Iran

Kayseri

*Lake
Tuz*

Malatya

Diyarbakir

*Lake
Van*

Van

Tabriz

Rasht

Mashhad

3

Adana

Gaziantep

Orumiyeh

*Lake
Urmia*

**TAURUS MOUNTAINS**

Mersin

Aleppo

Mosul

Irbil

**TEHRAN** ★

▲ Mount
Damavand
5671m

AFGHANISTAN

Iran

4

★ **NICOSIA**

**RUS**

Homs

**SYRIA**

*Tigris*

Kirkuk

Hamadan

Qom

**DASHT-E KAVIR**

Kuwait

**LEBANON**

**IRAQ**

Kermanshah

Arak

**I R A N**

**BEIRUT** ★

*Euphrates*

★**DAMASCUS**

**SYRIAN**

**BAGHDAD** ★

Esfahan

Yazd

**ZAGROS MOUNTAINS**

**DASHT-E LUT**

Bahrain

5

*nean*

*a*

**WEST BANK**

*DESERT*

Karbala

An Najaf

Al Kut

**IRANIAN
PLATEAU**

Kerman

Qatar

USALEM

★ ★**AMMAN**

*Dead
Sea*

An Nasiriyah

Ahvaz

Zahedan

**ISRAEL**

◇ Petra

Basra

Shiraz

6

A STRIP

**JORDAN**

**KUWAIT**
★**KUWAIT**

Bandar-e Bushehr

E

*R
e
d*

Tabuk

**AN
NAFUD**

**The Gulf**

Bandar-e
'Abbas

PAKISTAN

7

EGYPT

**A R A B I A N**

Buraydah

**AD DAHNA**

Ad Damman

**BAHRAIN**
**MANAMA**
**QATAR**

Dubai

*Strait of Hormuz*

**OMAN**

*Gulf of Oman*

N

Israel

Al Hufuf

★ **DOHA**

Suhar

8

*Red Sea*

**SAUDI**

Medina

**ARABIA**

★ **RIYADH**

*Tropic of Cancer*

**ABU DHABI**

**UNITED ARAB
EMIRATES**

As Sib

'Ibri

★ **MUSCAT**

Jordan

United Arab
Emirates

9

**P E N I N S U L A**

Jedda

Mecca

At Taif

Saudi Arabia

**AR RUB' AL KHALI
(EMPTY QUARTER)**

**O M A N**

*Arabian Sea*

The dromedary is used for milk, meat and to carry heavy loads. These camels are well suited to desert life and can go for many days without drinking water.

10

**Did you know?**

◇ The world's earliest civilizations developed in Mesopotamia, which is now Iraq.

Abha

Salalah

**Y E M E N**

SANA ★

Hodeida

Oman

11

Ta'izz

Al Mukalla

Yemen

*Socotra
(to Yemen)*

0      200      400 kilometres

12

Aden

Al Mandeb

*Gulf of Aden*

0      200      400 miles

Where can you find water you can't sink in?
The Dead Sea

# Central Asia

ASIA

The Pamirs, in the southeast of this region, form the second-highest mountain range in the world. Mountains also cover most of Kyrgyzstan and Tajikistan and much of Afghanistan. Kazakhstan has open grasslands, and further south in Uzbekistan and Turkmenistan there is a lot of sandy desert. Central Asia is land-locked, which means that it is cut off from the sea, although it has a huge inland lake called the Caspian Sea. This area gets very little rain, and winters and summers have extreme temperatures. There are few large cities and most people live in rural areas. Most of the farming is around the fertile river valleys at the base of the mountains and in Kazakhstan. The main crops include cotton, peaches, melons and apricots. Central Asia has large deposits of oil, coal and natural gas, and minerals such as iron and copper. Industries are mostly traditional ones, and some areas specialize in making carpets and leather goods.

### Country File

Afghanistan

Kazakhstan

Kyrgyzstan

Tajikistan

Turkmenistan

Uzbekistan

**Did you know?**

◈ There are huge reserves of coal in Central Asia. It is used mostly to fuel power stations.

Ural'sk

RUSSIAN FEDERATION

*Caspian Depression*

Atyrau

Aktau

*Caspian Sea*

Turkmenbasy

Balkanabat

**Did you know?**

◈ The Caspian Sea, in the west, is the largest saltwater lake in the world. It takes up an area of 371,000 sq km.

## Aral Sea

The Aral Sea once covered 68,000 square kilometres. But since 1960, it has shrunk to a quarter of its size because water from rivers that flow into the lake is being diverted to use for irrigation. Old ships that used to float on the lake are now sitting on dry land.

## Samarqand

One of the oldest cities in Central Asia is Samarqand, which contains some of the finest buildings in this area. They include several Islamic schools called madrasahs. Shirdar madrasah, shown here, was built in the early 1600s. It is decorated with millions of tiles.

## Snow leopard

The snow leopard lives high in the mountains of Central Asia. This big cat has very thick fur, which can be up to 10 centimetres long.

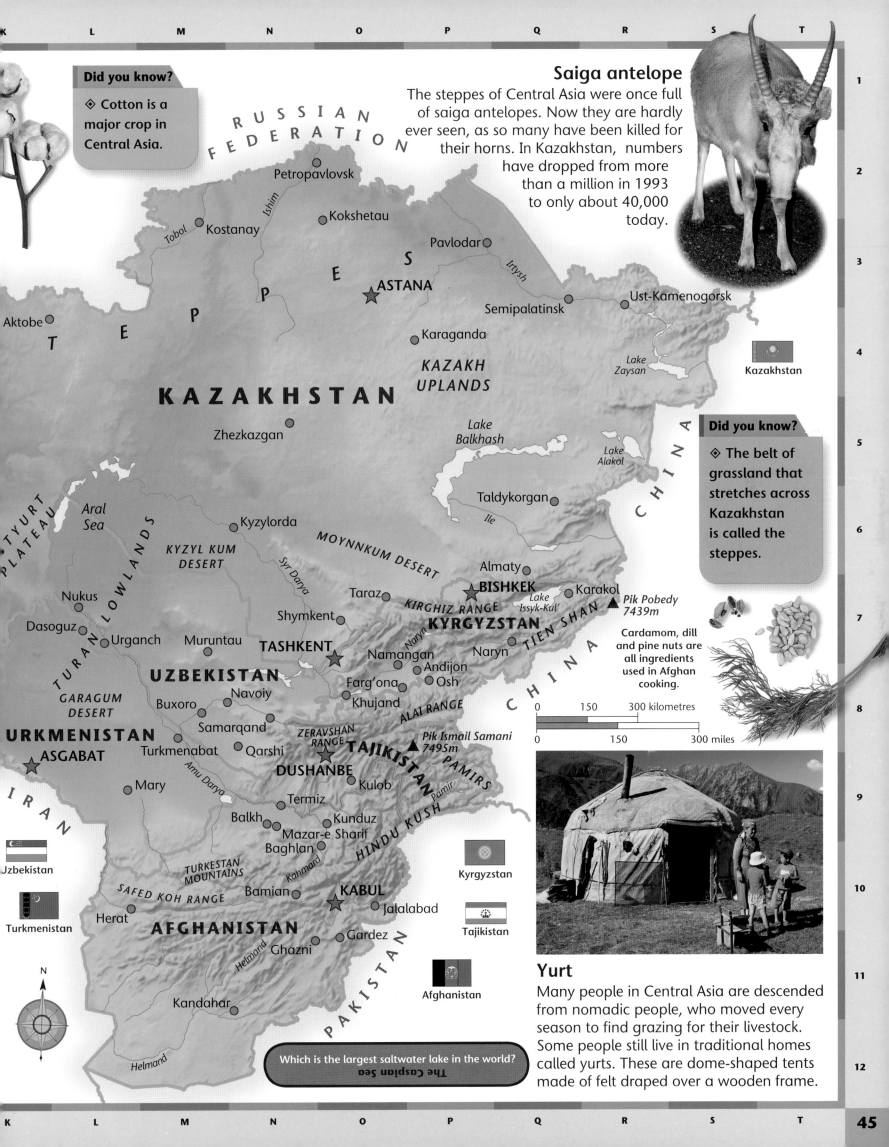

RUSSIAN FEDERATION

**Did you know?**

◈ Cotton is a major crop in Central Asia.

## Saiga antelope

The steppes of Central Asia were once full of saiga antelopes. Now they are hardly ever seen, as so many have been killed for their horns. In Kazakhstan, numbers have dropped from more than a million in 1993 to only about 40,000 today.

Petropavlovsk

Kostanay
Kokshetau
Tobol
Ishim

Pavlodar
Irtysh

★ ASTANA

Semipalatinsk
Ust-Kamenogorsk

Aktobe

Karaganda

**KAZAKH UPLANDS**

Kazakhstan

# KAZAKHSTAN

Zhezkazgan

Lake Balkhash

Lake Alakol

**Did you know?**

◈ The belt of grassland that stretches across Kazakhstan is called the steppes.

Lake Zaysan

Aral Sea

TYURT PLATEAU

Kyzylorda

KYZYL KUM DESERT

Taldykorgan
Ile

MOYNNKUM DESERT

CHINA

Nukus

TURAN LOWLANDS

Syr Darya

Almaty

Taraz

Karakol

★ BISHKEK

Lake Issyk-Kul'

Pik Pobedy 7439m

Dasoguz

Urganch

Muruntau

Shymkent

KIRGHIZ RANGE

TIEN SHAN

**KYRGYZSTAN**

Cardamom, dill and pine nuts are all ingredients used in Afghan cooking.

**TASHKENT** ★

Namangan
Andijon
Naryn

CHINA

# UZBEKISTAN

Navoiy

Farg'ona
Osh

Khujand

ALAI RANGE

GARAGUM DESERT

Buxoro

Samarqand

ZERAVSHAN RANGE

Pik Ismail Samani 7495m

0        150        300 kilometres

0        150        300 miles

URKMENISTAN

Turkmenabat

Qarshi

**TAJIKISTAN** ▲

PAMIRS

★ ASGABAT

**DUSHANBE**

Kulob

Pamir

Mary

Amu Darya

Termiz

IRAN

Balkh

Kunduz

Mazar-e Sharif

Baghlan

HINDU KUSH

Uzbekistan

TURKESTAN MOUNTAINS

Kahmard

Kyrgyzstan

Turkmenistan

SAFED KOH RANGE

Bamian

★ **KABUL**

Jalalabad

Tajikistan

Herat

# AFGHANISTAN

Gardez

Ghazni

Helmand

Afghanistan

## Yurt

Many people in Central Asia are descended from nomadic people, who moved every season to find grazing for their livestock. Some people still live in traditional homes called yurts. These are dome-shaped tents made of felt draped over a wooden frame.

Kandahar

PAKISTAN

N

Helmand

Which is the largest saltwater lake in the world?
The Caspian Sea

# South Asia
ASIA

This area is also called the Indian subcontinent. South Asia is separated from the rest of Asia by the towering peaks of the Himalayas. The tops of these mountains are always covered in snow. In the south there are lush tropical rainforests, and in the west are huge areas of desert. India has a typical monsoon climate. From March to June it is hot and dry. The wet season is from June to September, when large amounts of rain fall, often causing floods. October to February is cool and dry. Over one-fifth of the world's population lives in this area. After centuries of invasion and occupation, people have a rich variety of cultures and religions, and thousands of languages are spoken. Nearly two-thirds of the population work in agriculture, although most farmers grow only enough for their family. Rice grows in the wetter areas of the east and west, and millet and corn grow on higher areas inland. Tea is an important crop, especially in southwest India and Sri Lanka.

### Country File

Bangladesh

Bhutan

India

Maldives

Nepal

Pakistan

Sri Lanka

The population of India is the second-biggest in the world. There are now about 1.2 billion people living in India.

Pakistan

### Did you know?

◈ Bangladesh is one of the most densely populated countries in the world, and its population is one of the poorest. Most people survive by growing their own food.

## Bollywood

Filmmaking in India is a huge industry and it is known as "Bollywood." The films often contain spectacular song-and-dance routines, with expert fight scenes and beautiful heroes and heroines. Bollywood is based in the city of Mumbai, which used to be called Bombay.

### Did you know?

◈ The River Ganges is sacred to people who follow the Hindu religion, and it is worshipped as a goddess.

A cobra rears up and spreads its hood when it is alarmed.

## Taj Mahal

The Mughal emperor Shah Jahan built the beautiful Taj Mahal in Agra, India, in memory of his favourite wife, Mumtaz Mahal. It took 22 years to build and was finished in 1648. The Taj Mahal consists of four buildings, one of which is a tomb containing the bodies of Shah Jahan and his wife.

## Tea plantations

Sri Lanka and parts of India have the ideal climate for growing tea. Only the youngest tea leaves are picked. These are then wilted, oxidized, rolled and dried to produce the tea that we use to make the popular drink.

N

(claimed by India)

**K2**
▲ 8611m

AKSAI CHIN
(administered by China,
claimed by India)

HINDU
KUSH

KARAKORAM RANGE

Indus

AFGHANISTAN

Peshawar

Srinagar

**ISLAMABAD** ☆

Rawalpindi

Chenab

Gujranwala

Lahore

Faisalabad

Amritsar

Quetta

Multan

Sutlej

Ludhiana

PAKISTAN

Shikarpur

Indus

Sukkur

THAR
DESERT

Hyderabad

Karachi

RANN OF
KACHCHH

Tropic of Cancer

Gulf of Kachchh

Rajkot

Ahmadabad

Vadodara

Narmada

Gulf of Khambat

Surat

Nashik

Kalyan

Mumbai

Pune

Solapur

Hyderabad

HIMALAYAS

DEMCHOK
(administered by China,
claimed by India)

Nepal

Delhi

Meerut

**NEW DELHI** ☆

Ghaziabad

Jaipur

Agra

Yamuna

Chambal

Allahabad

VINDHYA RANGE

Indore

Bhopal

Jabalpur

INDIA

Nagpur

Aurangabad

DECCAN

Godavari

Krishna

Hubli

**NEPAL**

Pokhara

Lalitpur

KATHMANDU ☆

Biratnagar

Ganges

Lucknow

Ghaghara

Kanpur

Varanasi

Patna

Ganges

Ranchi

Rajshahi

Jamshedpur

Haora

Kolkata

Mouths of the Ganges

Bhubaneshwar

EASTERN GHATS

Visakhapatnam

Vijayawada

C

H

I

N

A

(Much of this area
is claimed by China)

Mt Everest
▲ 8848m

THIMPHU ☆
**BHUTAN**

Guwahati

Brahmaputra

Imphal

**BANGLADESH**
**DHAKA** ☆

Khulna

Chittagong

BURMA
(MYANMAR)

Bhutan

Bay of
Bengal

Bangladesh

India

## Himalayas

The Himalayas include nine of the world's ten highest mountains, including Mt Everest. It reaches a height of 8,848 metres, which is the highest point on Earth.

WESTERN GHATS

Malabar Coast

Arabian
Sea

Cardamom
and star
anise are
used in
drinks, to
flavour
food and as
medicines.

MALDIVES

MALE' ☆

INDIAN OCEAN

Laccadive
Islands

Maldives

Coimbatore

Kochi

Bangalore

Mysore

Coromandel Coast

Chennai

Madurai

Palk Strait

Jaffna

Trincomalee

Gulf of
Mannar

**SRI
LANKA**

Negombo

**COLOMBO** ☆

Kandy

Galle

INDIAN OCEAN

0    200 km

0    200 miles

Sri Lanka
is the world's
second-largest exporter
of tea after Kenya.

Sri Lanka

**Did you know?**

◈ In 2004 an earthquake under the ocean caused huge waves, called tsunamis. These tsunamis killed more than 300,000 people in Sri Lanka, India and other countries.

Andaman
Islands
(to India)

Andaman Sea

Nicobar
Islands
(to India)

0        200        400 kilometres

0              200            400 miles

**Can you find the most sacred river in the world?**
The River Ganges.

1　2　3　4　5　6　7　8　9　10　11　12

# East Asia
ASIA

A large part of East Asia has a landscape of high mountains, desert or steppe land. In the southeast the land changes from mountains to wide river valleys and open plains. To the east is Japan, which has a rugged, mountainous landscape. Japan is one of the richest nations in the world. It does not have many natural resources, so it imports them. Japan is well known for making advanced electronic equipment. It is also a world leader in vehicle manufacturing. China and South Korea now have strong economies.

## Country File
China

Japan

Mongolia

North Korea

South Korea

Taiwan

KAZAKHSTAN

ALTAI MOUNTAINS

DZUNGARIAN BASIN

KYRGYZSTAN

TIEN SHAN

○ Urumqi

TAJIKISTAN

TARIM BASIN

PAKISTAN

(Claimed by India)

TAKLA MAKAN DESERT

▲ K2 8611m

KUNLUN MOUNTAINS    ALTUN SHAN    QILIAN Sh

QAIDAM BASIN

(Administered by China, claimed by India)

INDIA

(Administered by China, claimed by India)

PLATEAU OF TIBET

C

Salween

Tibet

Brahmaputra ○ Lhasa

NEPAL

HIMALAYAS

China

Mt Everest 8848m

BHUTAN    INDIA

## Great Wall of China
The Great Wall of China is one of the largest structures in the world. It starts east of Beijing, near the Chinese coast, and stretches inland for about 8,850 kilometres. The oldest sections were built in the 7th century BCE, but it was rebuilt and added to over many centuries. It was made to keep out invaders from the north, such as the Mongols.

Traditional herbal medicine, such as these wolf berries, has been used in China for over 4,500 years.

## Giant panda
These are among the most endangered animals in the world. There are only about 1,800 left in the wild. Pandas are classified as carnivores (meat eaters), but 99 per cent of their diet is bamboo. Pandas live in thick bamboo forests in central China and spend about 14 hours a day eating!

BURMA

## Yak
Wild yaks live high on the Plateau of Tibet. They stand 2 metres high at the shoulder. Thick coats keep them warm in the extreme cold.

## Mount Fuji
The majestic volcano Mount Fuji is Japan's highest point, at 3,776 metres. It is a symbol of Japan and has been an inspiration to artists and writers for thousands of years.

Mongolia

Japan

North Korea

South Korea

Taiwan

Sushi is a well-known Japanese food made from rice, seaweed and fish.

## Shanghai
Shanghai is a huge seaport and one of the largest industrial and commercial centres in China. The population is constantly growing, as people from all over China move there, attracted by its success and to find a job. Today Shanghai has a population of more than 24 million.

Where is the highest point in Japan?
Mount Fuji

RUSSIAN FEDERATION

Darhan
Erdenet
ULAN BATOR
Choybalsan
MONGOLIA
GOBI
INNER MONGOLIA
GREAT KHINGAN RANGE
Amur
Qiqihar
Harbin
Manchuria
Jilin
Changchun
Baotou
Hohhot
Fushun
Shenyang
Anshan
NORTH KOREA
Hamhung
Ch'ongjin
Sea of Japan
Hokkaido
Sapporo
Sendai
Wonsan
Yellow River
BEIJING
Datong
Tianjin
Tangshan
Dalian
P'YONGYANG
SOUTH KOREA
Inchon
SEOUL
JAPAN
TOKYO
Honshu
Mt. Fuji 3776m
Yokohama
Yinchuan
Great Wall of China
Shijiazhuang
Taiyuan
Kyoto
Kobe
Nagoya
Osaka
Taegu
Pusan
Okayama
Hiroshima
Fukuoka
Kitakyushu
Shikoku
Nagasaki
Kyushu
Kagoshima
ning
Lanzhou
Xianyang
Luoyang
Handan
Jinan
Yellow River
Xuzhou
Zhengzhou
Qingdao
Yellow Sea
Xi'an
NA
Nanjing
Hefei
Shanghai
SICHUAN BASIN
Three Gorges Reservoir
Wuhan
Hangzhou
East China Sea
ngdu
Chongqing
Nanchang
Changsha
Ryukyu Islands
Yangtze River
Guiyang
Fuzhou
ming
T'AIPEI
Xi Jiang River
T'aichung
Guangzhou
T'ainan
TAIWAN
Kaohsiung
Nanning
Macao
Hong Kong
ETNAM
Gulf of Tongking
South China Sea
Hainan Dao
0 200 400 kilometres
0 200 400 miles

49

## Country File

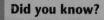

Brunei

Burma (Myanmar)

Cambodia

East Timor

Indonesia

Laos

Malaysia

Philippines

Singapore

Thailand

Vietnam

**Did you know?**

❖ The red gemstones called rubies are mined in Burma. Burmese rubies are known as the finest rubies in the world.

## Orangutan

These mammals are the only great apes in Asia and they are critically endangered. Their habitat is being destroyed and they are hunted for their young, which are sold as pets. Orangutans eat mostly fruit, but they also feed on leaves, shoots, insects and occasionally small animals and eggs.

**Did you know?**

❖ Angkor Wat in Cambodia is the world's largest religious monument. It dates back to 1113.

## Singapore

Singapore is a city-state made up of a main island (Singapore Island) and 62 other islands. It is the biggest port in Southeast Asia, one of the world's main oil-refining centres and a world leader in shipbuilding and repair. Singapore also has a thriving technology industry.

**Did you know?**

❖ In Singapore it is illegal to sell chewing gum or to drop litter.

## Paddy fields

People grow rice throughout Southeast Asia. Rice needs plenty of water and heat so this area's climate is ideal. Rice fields are called paddy fields. Each field has a low wall so that it can be flooded with water. On steep slopes the paddy fields are built in terraces.

**Did you know?**

❖ Siamese cats originally came from Thailand.

Burma

Hkakabo Razi 5885m ▲

INDIA

CHINA

Laos

Vietn

BANGLADESH

Chindwin

Irrawaddy

Tropic of Cancer

**BURMA**

Mandalay

*SHAN PLATEAU*

Meiktila

Taunggyi

Sittwe

Magwe

**NAYPYIDAW**

**HA NOI**

Hai Ph

Nam D

**LAOS**

Louangphabang

Prome

Vinh

Chiang Mai

**VIENTIANE**

Yangon

Pegu

**VIETNA**

Bassein

Moulmein

Udon Thani

Hué

Salween

Mekong

ANNAMESE CORDILLERA

Thailand

Bay of Bengal

*Mouths of the Irrawaddy*

*Gulf of Martaban*

**THAILAND**

Nakhon Ratchasima

Pakxé

Tavoy

Chon Buri

Angor Wat

*Tonle Sap*

Nho

Malaysia

**BANGKOK**

Batdambang

**CAMBODIA**

Trang

*Mergui Archipelago*

**PHNOM PENH**

Bien H

Ho Chi M

My Tho

Can Tho

*Gulf of Thailand*

Rach Gia

S o u t

*Isthmus of Kra*

*Ko Samui*

C h i n

Andaman Sea

*Phuket*

Hat Yai

Cambodia

S e a

Banda Aceh

Kuala Terengganu

Malay Peninsula

Ipoh

**KUALA LUMPUR**

Medan

*Lake Toba*

Klang

**M A L A**

*Strait of Malacca*

Johor Bahru

*Natuna Sea*

No
Is

Kuch

*Equator*

BARISAN MOUNTAINS

Pekanbaru

**SINGAPORE**

Sumatra

Pontianak

Padang

Jambi

*Bangka*

*Mentawai Islands*

INDIAN OCEAN

Bengkulu

I

Palembang

G r e a t

Bandarlampung

**JAKART**

Tangerang

Sem

Bogor

Bandung

Ja

Singapore

Yogyak

0 250 500 kilometres

0 250 500 m

6

7

8

9

10

11

12

# Southeast Asia

ASIA

Much of Southeast Asia is mountainous and covered in thick forest. This area has a tropical monsoon climate: half of the year is wet and half is dry. Most of the people live in the river valleys, on the fertile plains of the mainland or around the coasts of the islands. Some islands have no people living on them, but others, such as Java, have a big population. People in this area are from many different cultures. They follow many religions and speak hundreds of languages. The main industries are processing raw materials, such as oil, minerals, timber and food. Recently, the manufacturing of electronic goods and computers has increased.

**uddhism**

ne of the main religions in this area Buddhism. Like many Buddhist mples, this one is guarded y statues of lions t the entrance.

Luzon
Baguio
Philippine Sea
Philippines
MANILA
N
Mindoro
Samar
PHILIPPINES
Panay
Bacolod
Cebu
Palawan
Negros
Brunei
Sulu Sea
Cagayan de Oro
Mindanao
Zamboanga
Davao
Mount Kinabalu 4101m
ANDAR SERI GAWAN
Kota Kinabalu
Sandakan
Sulu Archipelago
RUNEI
Celebes Sea
PACIFIC OCEAN
I A
Manado
Halmahera
Borneo
Equator
East Timor
Samarinda
Palu
Molucca Sea
Balikpapan
Makassar Strait
Sulawesi
Jayapura
Papua
u n d a I s l a n d s
Ceram
O N E S I A
Buru
Banjarmasin
Kendari
Ambon
Puncak Jaya 4884m
CENTRAL RANGE
a Sea
Makassar
Banda Sea
Aru Islands
PAPUA NEW GUINEA
Flores Sea
Surabaya
Malang
Bali
Lesser Sunda Islands
Arafura Sea
Mataram
DILI
Denpasar
Flores
EAST TIMOR
Timor Sea
Sumbawa
Lombok
Sumba
Kupang
Timor
Indonesia

Lemongrass, lime and cilantro are important ingredients in Southeast Asian cooking.

### Komodo dragon

This is the world's largest lizard. It grows up to 3 metres long. Komodo dragons live on the Lesser Sunda Islands. Their teeth are serrated and their mouths are full of deadly bacteria. They are fierce predators and eat anything that they can overpower.

**Did you know?**

◈ The Sultan of Brunei has the largest palace in the world.

Unusual carved wooden masks like this one are worn by professional dancers in Indonesia.

**Did you know?**

◈ Indonesia is a group of 17,500 islands. This is called an "archipelago."

Can you find where the Komodo dragon lives?

The Lesser Sunda Islands, in Indonesia

# Australia

OCEANIA AND THE PACIFIC ISLANDS

This massive country is mostly desert, which is so hot and dry that it is not suitable for farming or for people to live there. The wildest, driest and emptiest parts of the Australian desert are sometimes called the outback. Most of the 22.5 million people in Australia live in towns along the coast, such as Brisbane, Melbourne and Sydney in the east and Perth in the southwest. The first inhabitants of this continent were the Aboriginal Australians. Today most Australians are descended from European people who migrated there from the 18th century onwards. Australia has one of the world's biggest mining industries. Copper, gold, coal and opals are all mined there. Other important Australian industries include tourism and winemaking.

**Country File**

Australia

3
4
5
6
11
12

**Did you know?**

◈ The world's longest fence is in Australia. It is 5,614 km long and was built to keep dingos away from sheep.

97 per cent of all opals are found in Australia.

INDIAN OCEAN

KIMBERLEY PLATEAU

Broome

GREAT SANDY DESERT

Port Hedland

Dampier

HAMERSLEY RANGE

GIBSON DESERT

Lake Mackay

Tropic of Capricorn

A U

WESTERN AUSTRALIA

GREA VICTOR DESER

Geraldton

Kalgoorlie

NULLA

Perth ☆
Fremantle

Mandurah

Bunbury

Cape Leeuwin

Albany

Great

SOUTHE

0    200    400 kilometres
0    200    400 mile

## Uluru

The magnificent rock called Uluru is the top of an enormous sandstone hill that is buried beneath the desert in Northern Territory. It is also known as Ayers Rock. This is the world's biggest single rock. Uluru rises nearly 350 metres above the surrounding land and it is 9.4 kilometres around the base. This ancient rock is a sacred place for many Aboriginal Australians.

## Kangaroo

Kangaroos are mammals called marsupials. The females carry their young in a pouch. Other marsupials in Australia are wallabies, possums and the koala. The only egg-laying mammals – the platypus and echidna – also live in Australia. They are called monotremes.

K L M N O P

Where can you find hundreds of coral reefs?
The Great Barrier Reef

**Did you know?**

◈ Australia is the only country that is also a continent on its own.

## Great Barrier Reef

The Great Barrier Reef is made up of over 2,800 coral reefs and is home to more than 1,500 species of fish. It covers an enormous area – 350,000 square kilometres.

Arafura Sea

Melville Island

Darwin

ARNHEM LAND

Gulf of Carpentaria

N

Cape York

CAPE YORK PENINSULA

Coral Sea

BARKLY TABLELAND

NAMI DESERT

NORTHERN TERRITORY

GREAT BARRIER REEF

Cairns

Townsville

Australia

Mackay

MACDONNELL RANGES

QUEENSLAND

Alice Springs

Rockhampton

T R A L I A

Gladstone

Uluru (Ayers Rock) 863m

SIMPSON DESERT

Hervey Bay

SOUTH AUSTRALIA

Lake Eyre North

Maroochydore-Mooloolaba

Sunshine Coast

Toowoomba

☆ Brisbane

Coober Pedy

Gold Coast

Lake Torrens

Lake Frome

## Koala

The koala lives in eucalyptus trees and eats the leaves. Many of these trees are being cut down to make more space for roads and buildings. Koalas are now endangered animals.

Lake Gairdner

FLINDERS RANGES

Darling River

NEW SOUTH WALES

GREAT DIVIDING RANGE

Coffs Harbour

an Bight

Port Macquarie

EAN

Broken Hill

Newcastle

Mildura

Bathurst

Adelaide ☆

Kangaroo Island

Murray River

Wagga Wagga

Albury

Mount Kosciuszko 2228m

Bendigo

VICTORIA

AUSTRALIAN ALPS

Ballarat

Geelong

☆ Melbourne

☆ Sydney

Nowra

Wollongong

★ CANBERRA

AUSTRALIAN CAPITAL TERRITORY

PACIFIC OCEAN

**Did you know?**

◈ The inland taipan has the strongest venom of any land snake. The venom in one bite could kill 100 people.

Bass Strait

Launceston

TASMANIA

☆ Hobart

## Sydney Opera House

Sydney is the biggest and oldest city in Australia, and the Sydney Opera House is one of the most famous buildings in the world. Over 100 million people have visited it.

# Pacific Islands

OCEANIA AND THE PACIFIC ISLANDS

There are thousands of islands in the Pacific Ocean. People from many cultures live there, speaking many languages. The islands are traditionally divided into these groups: Melanesia, Micronesia and Polynesia. The earliest people in this region settled on the island of New Guinea over 40,000 years ago. In the 19th century, the islands were colonized by Europeans, who brought their own cultures, languages and religions. Most of the islands are now part of independent countries. They rely on agriculture fishing for their income. The islands also export copra, which comes from coconuts. It is made into coconut oil, which is used in soap and cosmetics.

## Country File

Fiji

Kiribati

Marshall Islands

Micronesia

Nauru

Palau

Papua New Guinea

Samoa

Solomon Islands

Tonga

Tuvalu

Vanuatu

Onions, limes, ginger, garlic and lemon juice are all traditional ingredients of many south Pacific island dishes.

### Did you know?

◇ Nauru, in Micronesia, is the world's smallest republic. It has an area of only 21 sq km.

### Did you know?

◇ Most of the Pacific Islands were formed by volcanoes.

### Did you know?

◇ Papua New Guinea has more than 830 living languages.

◇ The coconut tree is called "the tree of life" by many islanders because every part of it is used or eaten.

*Tropic of Cancer*

NORTHERN MARIANA ISLANDS (to US)

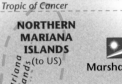 Marshall Isl

GUAM (to US)

 Micronesia   HAGATNA   Mi

MICRONESIA

*Yap*   *Chuuk Islands*   PALIKI

*Babeldaob*   *Pohnpei*

 Palau   OREOR   PALAU   *Caroline Island*

 Papua New Guinea   *Equator*   M

INDONESIA

PAPUA NEW GUINEA

▲ Mount Wilhelm 4509m   *New Britain*   S

PORT MORESBY   *Guadalcanal* HONIAR

*Coral Sea*

 Solomon Islands   CALED   (to

AUSTRALIA   *Tropic of Cap*

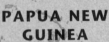 Vanuatu

## Fishing

The people of the Pacific islands fish mainly to feed themselves, but many fish are also caught in the northern Pacific by big fishing boats from Japan, South Korea, Taiwan and the USA. Tuna is a prized fish, and the finest tuna can sell for thousands of dollars per fish, especially in Japan. Today much of the commercial fishing of tuna is done using long fishing lines instead of nets.

## Doria's tree kangaroo

Nine of the 11 species of tree kangaroo live in the rainforest on the island of New Guinea. The other two live in Australia. Doria's tree kangaroo is the largest one, weighing up to 13 kilograms. Like all kangaroos, it is a marsupial.

## Papua New Guinea

New Guinea is the second-largest island in the world, and Papua New Guinea takes up the eastern half, as well as several smaller islands. About 80 per cent of the population lives in groups in the countryside. People live as they have done for many hundreds of years, with traditional ways of life, customs and beliefs.

## Cyclones

The Pacific islands suffer from cyclones every year. These strong winds blow at more than 120 kilometres per hour and can cause serious damage. In other parts of the world they are called typhoons or hurricanes. Palm trees can bend in the wind and survive cyclones.

*The International Date Line is an imaginary line that separates two calendar days. This means that the date to the east of the line is always one day ahead of the date to the west of the line.*

## Farming

Many Pacific islands are mountainous but people are able to grow some food crops along the coast. Coconuts, sweet potatoes and bananas all grow well in the hot, humid climate of the Pacific. Cocoa and coffee are important crops in Papua New Guinea.

## Green turtle

These endangered turtles live in warm waters all around the Pacific. They can reach 1.5 metres in length. The adults feed on sea grasses and algae, but the young eat jellyfish, shellfish and sponges.

### Did you know?

◈ In Papua New Guinea a language called Tok Pisin has developed, so that different communities can speak to each other.

## Polynesia

The beautiful island of Bora-Bora is in French Polynesia, a territory of France. Bora-Bora is one of the main tourist destinations of French Polynesia. Its highest peak is Mount Otemanu, which is 727 metres high.

Which country has more than 830 living languages?
Papua New Guinea

### Map labels

MIDWAY ISLANDS (to US)

WAKE ISLAND (to US)
Nauru
Tuvalu

Hawaiian Islands (to US)
Kauai
Oahu
Maui
Hawaii

JOHNSTON ATOLL (to US)

MARSHALL ISLANDS
Ratak Chain
Ralik Chain

Samoa

International Date Line

N

PACIFIC OCEAN

KINGMAN REEF (to US)
PALMYRA ATOLL (to US)
Line Islands
Kiritimati

BAKER & HOWLAND ISLANDS (to US)

Tarawa
BAIRIKI
Tungaru

Equator

JARVIS ISLAND (to US)

KIRIBATI
Phoenix Islands

KIRIBATI

P o l y n e s i a

TUVALU
Funafuti
FONGAFALE

TOKELAU (to New Zealand)

Santa Cruz Islands

WALLIS AND FUTUNA (to France)
Wallis
MATA'UTU
Futuna

SAMOA
APIA
AMERICAN SAMOA (to US)
PAGO PAGO

Northern Cook Islands

Millennium Island

Marquesas Islands

NUATU
Vanua Levu
Efate
PORT-VILA
Loyalty Islands
Noumea
NOUMÉA

Viti Levu
SUVA
Lau Group

TONGA

FIJI

NIUE (to New Zealand)
ALOFI

NUKU'ALOFA
Tongatapu

COOK ISLANDS (to New Zealand)

Bora-Bora
Southern Cook Islands
Society Islands
Tahiti
PAPEETE

Tuamotu Islands

FRENCH POLYNESIA (to France)

Rarotonga
AVARUA

Austral Islands

Gambier Islands

PITCAIRN ISLANDS (to UK)

NORFOLK ISLAND (to Australia)

Fiji

Tonga
Kiribati

0   250   500 kilometres
0   250   500 miles

Tasman Sea

NEW ZEALAND
North Island
WELLINGTON
South Island

# New Zealand

OCEANIA AND THE PACIFIC ISLANDS

**Country File**

New Zealand

This country in the south Pacific Ocean is about one quarter the size of Ontario. It consists of two main islands – North Island and South Island – and several smaller islands. New Zealand is known for its spectacular scenery. The landscape includes mountains, volcanoes, long sandy beaches, deep fjords and lush rainforests. It has cool, wet winters and warm, wet summers. New Zealand is one of the world's least populated countries, with 4.4 million people. The first people to settle there about 1,000 years ago were the Polynesians. They became known as the Maoris. For the past 160 years people have migrated there from many countries. Tourism, fishing and hi-tech manufacturing are important industries.

## Auckland

The largest city in New Zealand is Auckland. About one-third of the population lives there. Nearly 60 per cent of residents are descended from Europeans, and 11 per cent are Maori. Nobody in Auckland lives more than half an hour away from a beach.

**Did you know?**

◈ Almost one-third of New Zealand is covered by forest. Many of the forests contain unusual species of trees that are found only on these islands, such as kauri trees, which are some of the oldest trees on Earth.

This wooden Maori Tiki carving represents the first man. Tiki carvings are thought of as powerful good luck symbols.

## Whale-watching

One of the best places to see whales and dolphins in the wild is near the town of Kaikoura, on the east coast of South Island. New Zealand's whales, dolphins and seals are protected, and visitors from all over the world travel to Kaikoura to see them.

Tasman Sea

Westport

Greymouth

**South Island**

Aoraki/
Mount Cook
3724m ▲

Haast

Ashburton

Milford
Sound

SOUTHERN ALPS

Timaru

Wanaka

Waitaki

Canter...

Lake Wakatipu

Queenstown

Oamaru

Lake
Te Anau

FIORDLAND

Te Anau

Mataura

Clutha

Dunedin

Invercargill

Foveaux Strait

Stewart
Island

## Aoraki/Mount Cook

The highest mountain in New Zealand is Aoraki/ Mount Cook in the Southern Alps. It is 3,724 metres high. In Maori legend, these mountains are Aoraki and his three brothers, who are the sons of the Sky Father. They were stranded in their canoe and were frozen by the cold south wind. Their canoe became South Island.

*North Cape*

Apples and pears have been grown in the region around Nelson since the 1850s. Most of the fruit is exported to Europe.

**Did you know?**

◈ Aoraki/Mount Cook used to be about 10 m taller than it is now. In 1991 a huge amount of rock and ice fell off the summit in a landslide.

## Kiwi

The kiwi is the national symbol of New Zealand. This bird is about the size of a chicken. It cannot fly, so it is at risk from predators, especially domestic cats and dogs. There are only about 70,000 of these birds left in the wild.

Whangarei

*Great Barrier Island*

```
0        100        200 kilometres
0        100        200 miles
```

Auckland
Manurewa

*Bay of Plenty*

Hamilton
Tauranga

*Lake Rotorua*

*East Cape*

Rotorua
Whakatane

*Lake Taupo*
Taupo

New Plymouth

*North Island*

Gisborne

*Cape Egmont*

▲ Mount Ruapehu 2797m

▲ Mount Taranaki 2518m

Wanganui

*Rangitikei*

Napier

Hastings

## Geysers and springs

The area around Rotorua on North Island is famous for its geysers, hot springs and boiling mud, which are all heated deep inside the Earth. Geysers have a spiritual meaning for the Maoris and almost all have names. The largest is Pohutu, which shoots up to 30 metres into the air.

**N E W**

*e vell*

**Z E A L A N D**

Masterton

Lower Hutt
★ WELLINGTON

*n*

*nheim*

*Wairau*

*Cook Strait*

*Cape Palliser*

*Clarence*

Kairkoura

*P A C I F I C   O C E A N*

N

New Zealand

*Waimakariri*
*ristchurch*

*Banks Peninsula*

**Did you know?**

◈ Just over half of New Zealand's energy comes from hydroelectricity, which is produced by its fast-flowing rivers. The water is used to turn huge wheels called turbines, which in turn power an electric generator.

## Milford Sound

One of the most beautiful places in New Zealand is Milford Sound in the fjord lands of South Island. It is over 15 kilometres long and is surrounded by sheer cliffs rising more than 1,200 metres on each side. There are lush rainforests clinging to the sides of the fjord, and seals, dolphins and penguins swim in the waters.

There are about 40 million sheep in New Zealand. New Zealand lamb is famous all over the world.

## Hooker's sea lion

These sea lions are found only in New Zealand, mostly around the Auckland Islands. In the breeding season, a male lives with a group of up to 25 females. These sea lions can swim over 125 kilometres to find food, which includes squid, crabs, crayfish and fish.

In which area can you find many geysers?
In Rotorua, on North Island

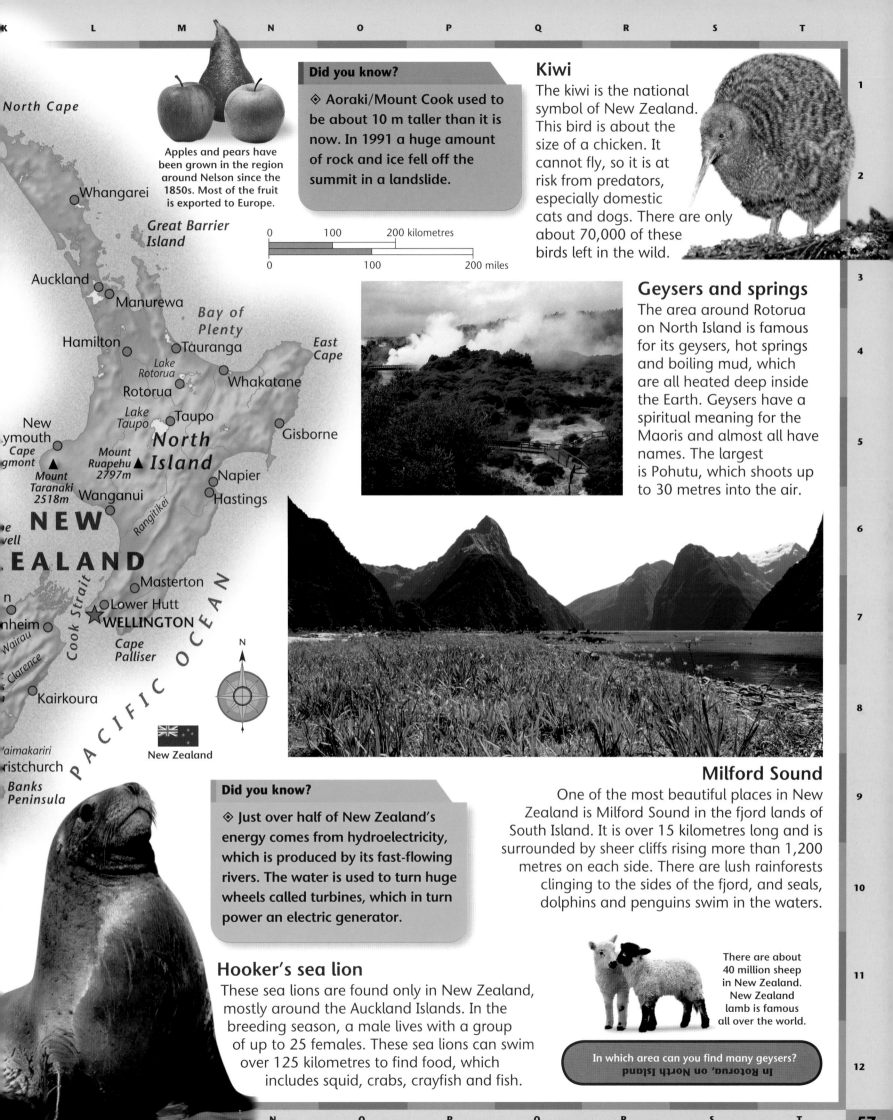

2

3

8

9

10

11

12

Limit of summer pack ice
Arctic Circle
Bering Strait
USA (Alaska)
Chukchi Sea
Wrangel Island
Limit of permanent ice cap
East Siberian Sea
New Siberian Islands
Beaufort Sea
R U S S I A N   F E D E R A T I O N
Banks Island
Laptev Sea
Victoria Island
ARCTIC OCEAN
Melville Island
Taymyr Peninsula
Queen Elizabeth Islands
Severnaya Zemlya
North Pole
Ellesmere Island
Kara Sea
Qaanaaq
Franz Josef Land
Knud Rasmussen Land
Wandel Sea
Baffin Bay
Baffin Island
GREENLAND (to Denmark)
Limit of permanent ice cap
Novaya Zemlya
SVALBARD (to Norway)
Limit of summer pack ice
Limit of winter pack ice
Barents Sea
Davis Strait
Ilulissat
Aasiat
Sisimiut
Maniitsoq
NUUK
Kong Christian IX Land
Gunnbjørn Fjeld 3,700m
Ittoqqortoormiit
Greenland Sea
North Cape
Kola Peninsula
Qaqortoq
Tasiilaq
Norwegian Sea
NORWAY
FINLAND
Nunap Isua
Denmark Strait
Arctic Circle
REYKJAVIK ☆ ICELAND

C A N A D A

0　　400　　800 kilometres
0　　400　　800 miles

# The Arctic

ASIA, EUROPE AND NORTH AMERICA

The Arctic is a huge area with the North Pole at its centre. It is not a continent or a country but includes the Arctic Ocean and the most northern parts of Asia, North America and Europe. During winter, much of the Arctic Ocean is covered by pack ice about 4 metres thick. During the short summers, the ice melts and the area of pack ice shrinks. It grows again when winter returns and temperatures drop to −60°C. Even though the climate is cold, people have lived in the Arctic for thousands of years. The Sami and Inuit people were originally nomads who survived by herding animals and hunting. Today most people live in new towns, but some still live a traditional life.

### Polar bear

There are 20–25,000 polar bears in the Arctic. These animals are now a threatened species. As the Arctic pack ice continues to melt, polar bears are finding it difficult to hunt for food because they have to swim so far between the bits of ice. Many polar bears are dying as they search for food.

### Did you know?

◈ By 2030 the Arctic may have ice-free summers because so much ice is melting in summer and not refreezing in winter.

Inuit people once lived by fishing, herding and hunting whales, bears and seals.

### Northern lights

The *aurora borealis*, or the northern lights, are caused by solar winds reacting with the Earth's upper atmosphere. This colourful effect in the sky can also be seen around the South Pole, where it is known as the southern lights, or *aurora australis*.

# Antarctica

ANTARCTICA

This is the fifth-largest continent. It is almost one and a half times the size of Canada. Antarctica has a harsh, cold climate and is the windiest place on Earth. Almost all of Antarctica is covered with a sheet of ice. On average, the ice is 1.6 kilometres thick, and it is thousands of years old. The ice contains most of the fresh water on Earth. Under the ice, the land contains oil and other minerals, including gold, iron ore and coal. Huge blocks of ice often break off the edge of the sheet and float away as icebergs. To protect this wilderness and its wildlife, 46 nations have signed an agreement called the Antarctic Treaty. They agree not to carry out any mining or put a military station there. Antarctica is the only continent where people do not live all year round.

## Cold science

Groups of scientists, tourists and explorers are allowed to visit Antarctica. Many things are studied in Antarctica, including how plants and animals can survive there.

Humpbacks and other whales visit the icy seas of Antarctica. When a whale leaps out of the water it is known as breaching.

**Did you know?**

◈ The weight of the ice in Antarctica has pushed the land below sea level.

## Emperor penguin

The only penguins that breed in Antarctica during the bitter cold winter are emperor penguins. They weigh over 30 kilograms and are the tallest penguins, at 1.2 metres high. They walk up to 120 kilometres to their breeding grounds.

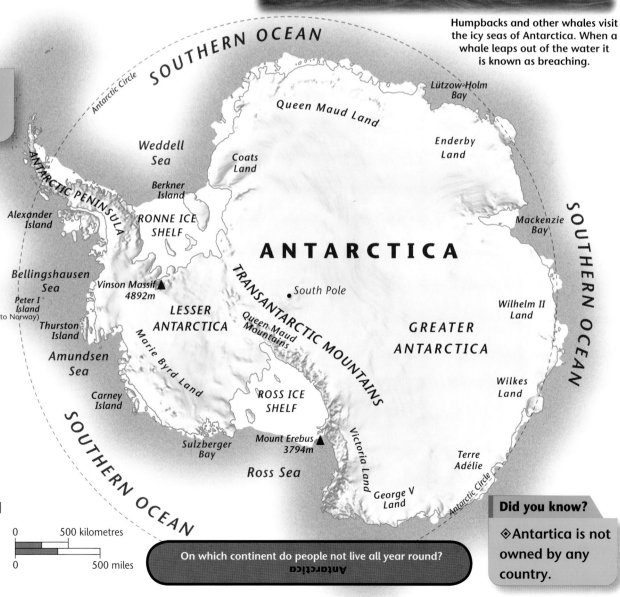

SOUTHERN OCEAN

Antarctic Circle

Lützow-Holm Bay

Queen Maud Land

Enderby Land

Weddell Sea

Coats Land

Berkner Island

ANTARCTIC PENINSULA

Alexander Island

RONNE ICE SHELF

Mackenzie Bay

**ANTARCTICA**

SOUTHERN OCEAN

Bellingshausen Sea

Vinson Massif ▲ 4892m

Peter I Island (to Norway)

South Pole

Wilhelm II Land

LESSER ANTARCTICA

Queen Maud Mountains

TRANSANTARCTIC MOUNTAINS

GREATER ANTARCTICA

Thurston Island

Amundsen Sea

Marie Byrd Land

Wilkes Land

Carney Island

ROSS ICE SHELF

Sulzberger Bay

Mount Erebus ▲ 3794m

Victoria Land

Terre Adélie

Ross Sea

George V Land

Antarctic Circle

SOUTHERN OCEAN

0 ———— 500 kilometres

0 ———— 500 miles

On which continent do people not live all year round?
Antarctica

**Did you know?**

◈ Antarctica is not owned by any country.

3

4

5

6

7

8

9

10

11

12

# Index to the maps

In this Atlas there is an **Index to the maps** on page 60 and a **General index** on page 68.

Place name index
The **Index to the maps** lists all the names that appear on the maps. Each name is followed by a description, its location, a page number and a grid reference number. Town names do not have a description.

place name   description   location

**Anatolia**   *physical region* Turkey **10 D5**

page number
grid reference

To find our example "Anatolia," first go to the page shown—p. 10, then find the letter "D" and number "5" around the border of the page. Trace a line down from "D" and a line across from "5." Where the lines meet directs you to the precise square on the grid in which "Anatolia" can be found.

• • A • •

**Aalborg**   Denmark **33 L10**
**Aasiat**   Greenland **58 B6**
**Aberdeen**   Scotland, UK **35 O2**
**Abha**   Saudi Arabia **43 N10**
**Abidjan**   Ivory Coast **28 H10**
**Abu Dhabi**   *capital city* United Arab Emirates **43 Q8**
**Abuja**   *capital city* Nigeria **28 J10**
**Acapulco**   Mexico **24 G8**
**Accra**   *capital city* Ghana **28 H10**
**Aconcagua, Cerro**   *mountain* Argentina **27 O9**
**A Coruña**   Spain **35 M8**
**Adana**   Turkey **43 L3**
**Ad Dahna**   *desert* Saudi Arabia **43 O7**
**Ad Damman**   Saudi Arabia **43 P7**
**Addis Ababa**   *capital city* Ethiopia **29 O9**
**Adelaide**   *state capital* South Australia **53 M9**
**Aden**   Yemen **43 N12**
**Aden, Gulf of**   *sea feature* NW Indian Ocean **10 E7**
**Adriatic Sea**   *sea* Mediterranean Sea **37 O8**
**Aegean Sea**   *sea* Mediterranean Sea **39 O10**
**Afghanistan**   *country* C Asia **45 M10**
**Africa**   *continent* **10 C7**
**Agadez**   Niger **28 J8**
**Agra**   India **47 N4**
**Ahaggar**   *plateau* Algeria **28 I7**
**Ahmadabad**   India **47 M6**
**Ahvaz**   Iran **43 O5**
**Ajaccio**   France **35 R9**
**Aksai Chin**   *disputed territory* S Asia **47 O1**
**Aktau**   Kazakhstan **44 I6**
**Aktobe**   Kazakhstan **45 K4**
**Akureyri**   Iceland **33 L1**
**Alabama**   *state* USA **23 P8**
**Alai Range**   *mountain range* Kyrgyzstan/Tajikistan **45 O8**
**Alakol, Lake**   *lake* Kazakhstan **45 R5**
**Aland Islands**   *island group* Finland **33 O8**

**Alaska**   *state* USA **22 G9**
**Alaska, Gulf of**   *sea feature* N Pacific Ocean **22 G10**
**Alaska Range**   *mountain range* USA **11 M3**
**Albacete**   Spain **35 O11**
**Albania**   *country* SE Europe **39 M9**
**Albany**   Western Australia **52 G10**
**Albany**   *state capital* New York, USA **23 R5**
**Alberta**   *province* Canada **20 H7**
**Albuquerque**   New Mexico, USA **23 K8**
**Albury**   New South Wales, Australia **53 O10**
**Aldan**   *river* Russia **41 O8**
**Aleppo**   Syria **43 L4**
**Aleutian Islands**   *island group* USA **11 L4**
**Alexander Island**   *island* Antarctica **59 N8**
**Alexandria**   Egypt **29 M5**
**Algeria**   *country* N Africa **28 I6**
**Algiers**   *capital city* Algeria **28 I4**
**Al Hufuf**   Saudi Arabia **43 P7**
**Alicante**   Spain **35 O11**
**Alice Springs**   Northern Territory, Australia **53 L6**
**Al Kut**   Iraq **43 O5**
**Allahabad**   India **47 O5**
**Almaty**   Kazakhstan **45 Q6**
**Al Mukalla**   Yemen **43 P11**
**Alofi**   *capital city* Niue **55 N8**
**Alps**   *mountain range* C Europe **10 C4**
**Altai Mountains**   *mountain range* C Asia **10 G4**
**Altamira**   Brazil **27 Q4**
**Altun Shan**   *mountain range* China **48 H6**
**Amazon**   *river* C South America **27 Q4**
**Amazon Basin**   *basin* C South America **27 O4**
**Ambon**   Indonesia **51 O10**
**American Samoa**   *US territory* C Pacific Ocean **55 N7**
**Amiens**   France **35 P5**
**Amman**   *capital city* Jordan **43 L5**
**Amritsar**   India **47 M3**
**Amsterdam**   *capital city* Netherlands **35 Q4**
**Amu Darya**   *river* C Asia **45 M9**
**Amundsen Sea**   *sea* Southern Ocean **59 N10**
**Amur**   *river* China/Russia **10 I4**
**Anápolis**   Brazil **27 Q6**
**Anatolia**   *physical region* Turkey **10 D5**
**Anchorage**   Alaska, USA **22 G10**
**Andaman Islands**   *island group* India **47 S9**
**Andaman Sea**   *sea* NE Indian Ocean **50 F7**
**Andes**   *mountain range* W South America **27 M5**
**Andijon**   Uzbekistan **45 P8**
**Andorra**   *country* SW Europe **35 O9**
**Andros Island**   *island* Bahamas **25 M6**
**Angara**   *river* Russia **41 K9**
**Angel Falls**   *waterfall* Venezuela **27 P3**
**Angkor Wat**   *archaeological site* Cambodia **50 I5**
**Angola**   *country* S Africa **30 I7**
**Anguilla**   *UK territory* Caribbean **25 R7**
**Ankara**   *capital city* Turkey **43 K2**
**An Nafud**   *desert* Saudi Arabia **43 M6**
**An Najaf**   Iraq **43 N5**
**Annamese Cordillera**   *mountain range* SE Asia **50 I4**
**Annapolis**   *state capital* Maryland, USA **23 R6**
**An Nasiriyah**   Iraq **43 O6**
**Anshan**   China **49 O5**
**Antalya**   Turkey **43 K3**
**Antananarivo**   *capital city* Madagascar **31 O8**
**Antarctica**   *continent* **59 P8**
**Antarctic Peninsula**   *peninsula* Antarctica **59 N8**
**Anticosti Island**   *island* Canada **21 Q8**
**Antigua & Barbuda**   *country* Caribbean **25 R7**
**Antofagasta**   Chile **27 N7**
**Antwerp**   Belgium **35 Q5**
**Aoraki**   *mountain* New Zealand **56 I9**
**Apennines**   *mountain range* Italy **37 M7**

**Apia**   *capital city* Samoa **55 N8**
**Appalachian Mountains**   *mountain range* USA **23 P7**
**Arabian Peninsula**   *peninsula* SW Asia **43 M7**
**Arabian Sea**   *sea* NW Indian Ocean **10 F6**
**Aracaju**   Brazil **27 S5**
**Arafura Sea**   *sea* SW Pacific Ocean **10 I8**
**Araguaia**   *river* Brazil **27 Q5**
**Arak**   Iran **43 P4**
**Aral Sea**   *lake* Kazakhstan/Uzbekistan **45 L6**
**Ararat, Mt**   *mountain* Turkey **43 N2**
**Aras**   *river* SW Asia **43 O3**
**Archangel**   Russia **40 G6**
**Arctic Ocean**   *ocean* **58 C3**
**Arequipa**   Peru **27 N6**
**Argentina**   *country* S South America **27 O9**
**Arhus**   Denmark **33 L10**
**Arica**   Chile **27 N6**
**Arizona**   *state* USA **22 I8**
**Arkansas**   *state* USA **23 N7**
**Arkansas**   *river* USA **23 N8**
**Armenia**   *country* SW Asia **43 N2**
**Arnhem Land**   *physical region* Australia **53 L2**
**Ar Rub' Al Khali**   *desert* Saudi Arabia **43 O9**
**Arta**   Greece **39 N10**
**Aruba**   *Dutch territory* Caribbean **25 P9**
**Aru Islands**   *island group* Indonesia **51 Q11**
**Ascension Island**   *UK territory* C Atlantic Ocean **12 A8**
**Ascension Island**   *island* C Atlantic Ocean **10 B8**
**Asgabat**   *capital city* Turkmenistan **45 K9**
**Ashburton**   New Zealand **56 J9**
**Asia**   *continent* **10 H4**
**Asmara**   *capital city* Eritrea **29 O8**
**As Sib**   Oman **43 R8**
**Astana**   *capital city* Kazakhstan **45 O3**
**Astrakhan'**   Russia **40 E9**
**Asunción**   *capital city* Paraguay **27 P7**
**Aswan**   Egypt **29 N7**
**Atacama Desert**   *desert* Chile **27 O7**
**Athabasca**   *river* Canada **20 H8**
**Athabasca, Lake**   *lake* Canada **20 I7**
**Athens**   *capital city* Greece **39 O10**
**Atlanta**   *state capital* Georgia, USA **23 P8**
**Atlantic Ocean**   *ocean* **10 B9**
**Atlas Mountains**   *mountain range* NW Africa **28 H5**
**At Taif**   Saudi Arabia **43 M9**
**Atyrau**   Kazakhstan **44 J5**
**Auckland**   New Zealand **57 L3**
**Augusta**   *state capital* Maine, USA **23 S4**
**Aurangabad**   India **47 M7**
**Austin**   *state capital* Texas, USA **23 M9**
**Austral Islands**   *island group* French Polynesia **55 P9**
**Australia**   *country* **52 J6**
**Australia**   *continent* **10 I9**
**Australian Alps**   *mountain range* Australia **53 O10**
**Australian Capital Territory**   *territory* Australia **53 P10**
**Austria**   *country* C Europe **37 O5**
**Avarua**   *capital city* Cook Islands **55 O9**
**Ayers Rock**   *see* Uluru
**Azerbaijan**   *country* SW Asia **43 O2**
**Azores**   *island group* Portugal **34 I11**
**Azov, Sea of**   *sea* Black Sea **39 S6**

• • B • •

**Babeldaob**   *island* Palau **54 H5**
**Bab el Mandeb**   *sea feature* NW Indian Ocean **43 N12**
**Babruysk**   Belarus **39 P2**
**Bacau**   Romania **39 P6**
**Bacolod**   Philippines **51 N6**
**Baffin Bay**   *sea feature* NW Atlantic Ocean **58 B5**
**Baffin Island**   *island* Canada **21 M4**
**Baghdad**   *capital city* Iraq **43 N5**
**Baghlan**   Afghanistan **45 O10**

**Baguio**   Philippines **51 M4**
**Bahamas**   *country* Caribbean **25 N6**
**Bahamas**   *island group* Caribbean **11 Q6**
**Bahía Blanca**   Argentina **27 P10**
**Bahrain**   *country* SW Asia **43 P7**
**Baikal, Lake**   *lake* Russia **41 L10**
**Bairiki**   *capital city* Kiribati **55 L6**
**Baja California**   *peninsula* Mexico **24 D3**
**Baker & Howland Islands**   *US territory* C Pacific Ocean **55 M6**
**Baku**   *capital city* Azerbaijan **43 P2**
**Balearic Islands**   *island group* Spain **35 P11**
**Bali**   *island* Indonesia **51 L11**
**Balikpapan**   Indonesia **51 L9**
**Balkanabat**   Turkmenistan **44 J8**
**Balkan Mountains**   *mountain range* Bulgaria **39 O8**
**Balkh**   Afghanistan **45 N9**
**Balkhash, Lake**   *lake* Kazakhstan **45 P5**
**Ballarat**   Victoria, Australia **53 N10**
**Balsas**   *river* Mexico **24 G7**
**Baltic Sea**   *sea* NE Atlantic Ocean **33 O11**
**Baltimore**   Maryland, USA **23 R6**
**Bamako**   *capital city* Mali **28 G9**
**Bamian**   Afghanistan **45 N10**
**Banda Aceh**   Indonesia **50 F7**
**Bandar Seri Begawan**   *capital city* Brunei **51 L8**
**Bandar-e' Abbas**   Iran **43 R7**
**Bandar-e Bushehr**   Iran **43 P6**
**Bandarlampung**   Indonesia **50 I10**
**Banda Sea**   *sea* W Pacific Ocean **51 O10**
**Bandung**   Indonesia **50 J11**
**Bangalore**   India **47 N9**
**Bangka**   *island* Indonesia **50 I9**
**Bangkok**   *capital city* Thailand **50 H5**
**Bangladesh**   *country* S Asia **47 R5**
**Bangui**   *capital city* Central African Republic **29 L10**
**Banja Luka**   Bosnia & Herzegovina **39 L7**
**Banjarmasin**   Indonesia **51 L10**
**Banjul**   *capital city* Gambia **28 F9**
**Banks Island**   *island* Canada **20 I3**
**Banks Peninsula**   *peninsula* New Zealand **57 K9**
**Banska Bystrica**   Slovakia **37 Q5**
**Baotou**   China **49 M6**
**Barbados**   *country* Caribbean **25 S8**
**Barcelona**   Spain **35 P9**
**Barcelona**   Venezuela **27 O2**
**Barents Sea**   *sea* Arctic Ocean **58 E6**
**Bari**   Italy **37 P9**
**Barinas**   Venezuela **27 N2**
**Barisan Mountains**   *mountain range* Indonesia **50 G8**
**Barkley Tableland**   *plateau* Australia **53 L3**
**Barnaul**   Russia **40 J10**
**Barquisimeto**   Venezuela **27 N2**
**Barranquilla**   Colombia **27 N2**
**Basel**   Switzerland **37 L5**
**Basra**   Iraq **43 O6**
**Bassein**   Burma **50 F4**
**Bass Strait**   *sea feature* Australia **53 O11**
**Batdambang**   Cambodia **50 I5**
**Bathurst**   New South Wales, Australia **53 P9**
**Baton Rouge**   *state capital* Louisiana, USA **23 O9**
**Beaufort Sea**   *sea* Arctic Ocean **58 B2**
**Beijing**   *capital city* China **49 N6**
**Beira**   Mozambique **31 M9**
**Beirut**   *capital city* Lebanon **43 L4**
**Belarus**   *country* E Europe **39 P2**
**Belém**   Brazil **27 R4**
**Belfast**   *province capital* Northern Ireland, UK **35 N3**
**Belgium**   *country* NW Europe **35 Q5**
**Belgrade**   *capital city* Serbia **39 M7**
**Belize**   *country* Central America **25 K8**
**Belize City**   Belize **25 K8**
**Bellingshausen Sea**   *sea* Southern Ocean **59 N9**
**Belmopan**   *capital city* Belize **25 K8**
**Belo Horizonte**   Brazil **27 R7**

# General index

The **General index** lists all the main topics that you can read about in this book and tells you the pages where they can be found.

# Picture sources

The publisher would like to thank the following individuals and organizations for their permission to use their photographs:

**Abbreviations**
t = top; b = bottom; c = centre;
r = right; l = left.

Aloysius Han - www.geohavens. com for the rubies on p50; Alstom; Automobili Lamborghini SpA; CN Tower, Canada; Dickinson by Design; Ford Motor Company; International Crane Foundation, Baraboo, Wisconsin; Jumeirah International; Memories of New Zealand -www. memoriesofnz.co.nz; Saab Great Britain Ltd

**Ardea**: John Wombe/Auscape/ Ardea. com 53 bc

**Britain on View**: www.britainonview. com 34 bc

**Bruce Coleman**: 55 cr

**Corbis**: Tiziana and Gianni Baldizzone: 32 tr; Sharna Balfour; Gallo Images: 31 tr; Tom Bean: 36 bl; Fernando Bengoechea/Beateworks: 35 tr; Tibor Bognar: 46 cl, 46 cl; Christophe Boisvieux: 17 br; Simonpietri Christian/ Corbis Sygma: 9 br; Arko Datta/Reuters: 46 cl; Colin Dixon/ Arcaid: 38 crb; DLILLC: 30 bc, 56 cr; epa: 14 cl; Alejandro Ernesto/epa: 14 bl; Randy Faris: 24 bl; Paddy Fields - Louie Psihoyos: 50 bl; Franz Marc Frei: 56 bl; Natalie Fobes: 35 br; Owen Franken: 17 tr; Darrell Gulin: 15 tr; Ainal Abd Halim/Reuters: 42 tr; Lindsay Hebberd: 17 tl; Chris Hellier: 31 cr; Dallas and John Heaton/ Free Agents Limited: 29 br, 49 tr; Jon Hicks: 27 br; Robert van der Hilst: 38 cl; Eric and David Hosking: 15 bcl; Hanan Isachar: 43 tr; Wolfgang Kaehler: 15 tl,15 br, 54 bl; Catherine Karnow: 38 cr, 55 tr; Frank Krahmer/ zefa: 27 cl; Jacques Langevin/Corbis Sygma: 41 tr; Danny Lehman: 25 br; John and Lisa Merrill: 36 c; Viviane Moos: 46 tr; Kazuyoshi Nomachi: 29 tc; Neil Rabinowitz: 57 cr; Finbarr O'Reilly/ Reuters: 16 tr; José Fuste Raga/zefa: 14 br, 22 bl, 34 cr, 49 br, 50 c; Carmen Redondo: 32 br; Reuters: 26 cr, 53 tr; Guenter Rossenbach/zefa: 15 tcl; Galen Rowell: 55 tl, 58 cr; Anders Ryman: 52 cl; Kevin Schafer: 9 bc; Alfio Scigliano/ Sygma/Corbis: 37 br; Paul Seheult/ Eye Ubiquitous: 26 tr, Hugh Sitton/ zefa: 51 tl; Hubert Stadler: 15 tcr; Paul A. Souders: 33 cr; Jon Sparks: 42 bl; Shannon Stapleton/Reuters: 16 bl; Hans Strand: 56 tr; Staffan Widstrand: 37 cr; Uli Wiesmeier/zefa: 36 tr; Tony Wharton/ Frank Lane Picture Agency: 37 tr; Larry Williams: 25 tr; Valdrin Xhemaj/epa: 21 tc; Shamil Zhumatov/Reuters: 44 c.

**ESA**: 8 cl, c, cr, 9 cl, c, ca, cr.

**FLPA**: Ingo Arndt/Foto Natural/Minden Pictures: 38 bc; Richard Becker: 14 tr; Jim Brandenburg/Minden Pictures: 48 cl; Hans Dieter Brandl: 32 cr; Michael Callan: 32 cl; R.Dirscherl: 51 cr;

Gerry Ellis/Minden Pictures: 48 bl; im Fitzharris/Minden Pictures/FLPA: 20 bl; Michael & Patricia Fogden/Minden Pictures: 24 bc; Michael Gore: 52 c; Rev. Bruce Henry: 46 br; Michio Hoshino/Minden Pictures: 23 tr, 58 br; Mitsuaki Iwago /Minden Pictures: 52 bc; Frank W Lane: 45 tr; Frans Lanting: 23 bc, 26 bc, 29 cr; Thomas Mangelsen/ Minden Picture: 4-5 b; S & D & K Maslowski: 20 bc; Claus Meyer/Minden Pictures: 26 cl; Yva Momatiuk /Minden Pictures: 27 tr; Colin Monteath /Minden Pictures: 47 tr; Rinie van Muers/Foto Natura: 3 c, 59 tr; Mark Newman: 41 tl; Flip Nicklin/Minden Picture: 21 tr; R & M Van Nostrand: 28 bl; Alan Parker: 44 bl; Walter Rohdich: 46 cr; L Lee Rue: 21 cr; Cyril Ruoso \JH Editorial/Minden Pictures: 36 br; Silvestris Fotoservice: 39 cr; Jurgen & Christine Sohns: 31 tc, 44 br; Inga Spence: 42 bc; Egmont Strigl/ Imagebroker/FLPA: 45 br; Chris & Tilde Stuart: 43 br; Terry Andrewartha: 58 tr; Barbara Todd/ Hedgehog House/ Minden Pictures: 59 cr; Winfried Wisniewski: 40 cl, 59 bl; Terry Whittaker: 34 tr; Konrad Wothe/Minden Pictures: 40 bc; Zhinong Xi/Minden Pictures: 49 tl; Shin Yoshino/Minden Pictures: 53 cr.

**Andy Crawford**: 51 br

**Steve Gorton**: 24 c, 34 cl, 36 c, 38 tc, bc, 41 bl, 42 c, 45 tl, cr, 47 cl, bc, 49 cr, 51 c, 54 tr, 54 tr, 54 bc

**NASA**: 9 tr, 23 br.
**Chez Picthall**: 2 b, 23 tc, 41 br.

**Peter Picthall**: 28 cl

**Still Pictures**: K. Thomas/Still Pictures: 39 tl

**Warren Photographic**: Jane Burton: 39 br, 50 tr, 57 br; Kim Taylor and Mark Taylor: 32 c; Mark Taylor: 50 tl, Monarch butterflies © Warren Photographic: 24 tc.

**Dominic Zwemmer**: 14 cl, 15 bc, 30 cl, 53 br, 57 ac

**Front cover**
Main image: NASA; Keith Binns/ iStockphoto: tl; Michael Gore FLPA: cl; Dominic Zwemmer: clb; Cyril Ruoso\ JHEditoria/Minden Pictures/FLPA: bl

**Back cover**
WarrenPhotographic: tl; NASA: bl.

All other images © of Picthall and Gunzi.

**Every effort has been made to trace the copyright holders and we apologize in advance for any unintentional omissions. We would be pleased to insert the appropriate acknowledgement in any subsequent edition of this book.**

# Continents of the world

ATLANTIC
OCEAN

EUROPE

ASIA

AFRICA

ATLANTIC
OCEAN

INDIAN
OCEAN

AUST

SOUTHERN OCEAN